Principles and Practice of Assessment in the Lifelong Learning Sector

Ann Gravells

LearningMatters

First published in 2009 by Learning Matters Ltd.

British Library Cataloguing in Publication Data
A CIP record for this book is available from the British Library.

ISBN: 978 1 84445 196 8

Cover design by Topics – The Creative Partnership
Project management by Deer Park Productions, Tavistock, Devon
Typeset by Pantek Arts Ltd, Maidstone, Kent
Printed and bound in Great Britain by Bell & Bain Ltd, Glasgow

Learning Matters Ltd
33 Southernhay East
Exeter EX1 1NX
Tel: 01392 215560
info@learningmatters.co.uk
www.learningmatters.co.uk

CONTENTS

ACKNOWLEDGEMENTS

The author would like to thank the following for their support and encouragement whilst writing this book:

Sharron Carlill
Peter Frankish
Bob Gravells
Julia Morris
Susan Simpson
Clare Weaver
Joan Willison

The students and staff of the teacher/training department at Bishop Burton College.

The author and publisher would like to thank the following for permission to reproduce copyright material:

Lifelong Learning UK

Ann Gravells is a lecturer in teacher training at Bishop Burton College in East Yorkshire. She has 24 years' experience of teaching in further education.

She is a consultant to City & Guilds for various projects as well as externally verifying the City & Guilds teacher training qualifications and assessor awards.

Ann holds a Masters in Educational Management, a PGCE, a Degree in Education, and a City & Guilds Medal of Excellence for teaching. She is the author of *Preparing to Teach in the Lifelong Learning Sector* and co-author of *Planning and Enabling Learning in the Lifelong Learning Sector* and *Equality and Diversity in the Lifelong Learning Sector*.

Ann is a Fellow of the Institute for Learning and a Member of the Chartered Institute for Educational Assessors.

The author welcomes any comments from readers; please e-mail consult@anngravells.co.uk

In this chapter you will learn about:

- the structure of the book and how to use it;
- Lifelong Learning professional teaching standards;
- National Vocational Qualifications (NVQs) and the A1 and A2 Awards.

The structure of the book and how to use it

This book has been specifically written for teachers and assessors who are working towards the Certificate in Teaching in the Lifelong Learning Sector (CTLLS) and/or the Learning and Development Assessor Awards (A1 and A2). Principles and Practice of Assessment is a core unit of the CTLLS qualification; however, the content is applicable to anyone requiring further information to assist their role as an assessor, or for continuing professional development (CPD).

The book is structured in chapters which relate to the content of the qualifications. You can work logically through the book or just look up relevant aspects within the chapters. The contents build upon the information in the companion books by Gravells (2008) *Preparing to Teach in the Lifelong Learning Sector*, and Gravells and Simpson (2008) *Planning and Enabling Learning in the Lifelong Learning Sector*.

There are activities to enable you to think about how you assess, and examples to help you understand the subject of assessment.

At the end of each chapter is a reference and further information list, enabling you to research relevant topics further, by using text books, publications and/or the internet.

Each chapter is cross referenced to the new overarching professional standards for teachers, tutors and trainers in the Lifelong Learning Sector, and the Learning and Development Assessor A1 and A2 Awards. If you are taking an Assessment qualification, particularly at level 4, you will be required to use academic writing and research skills, and reference your work to other sources besides this text.

Chapter 7 contains sample documents and pro-formas that you might wish to use when assessing.

The appendices contain the qualification criteria, a useful list of relevant abbreviations and acronyms, and an assessor checklist.

The index will help you to quickly locate useful topics.

Lifelong Learning professional teaching standards

In September 2007 professional standards came into effect for all new teachers in the Lifelong Learning Sector who teach on government funded programmes in England.

The full standards encompass six domains:

A Professional Values and Practice;

B Learning and Teaching;

C Specialist Learning and Teaching;

D Planning for Learning;

E Assessment for Learning;

F Access and Progression.

The standards can be accessed via the Lifelong Learning UK (LLUK) website (www.lluk.org) or by using the shortcut: http://tinyurl.com/5mmg9s.

As you progress through the teaching qualifications, you will need to meet all the relevant criteria relating to the *scope, knowledge* and *practice* required in your job role (referenced by: S for *scope*, K for *knowledge* or P for *practice* within the chapters).

The new qualifications have been developed based upon the Qualifications and Credit Framework (QCF) model, which has mandatory and optional units at different levels, and with different credit values. The units and credits can be built up to form relevant qualifications over time. Principles and Practice of Assessment is a three credit unit, available at levels 3 and 4 and can be found in Appendix 1.

The QCF is currently being phased in (in England, Wales and Northern Ireland) and has nine levels: entry, plus 1 to 8. The framework helps learners compare the requirements at each level, and identify a suitable progression route.

Each unit has a credit value which represents ten hours, showing how much time it takes to complete a unit. There are three sizes of qualifications:

● Awards (1 to 12 credits);

● Certificates (13 to 36 credits);

● Diplomas (37 credits or more).

By looking at the title and level of a unit or qualification, learners will be able to see how difficult it is and how long it will take to complete. A comparison of the levels to existing qualifications is:

● level 1– GCSEs (grades D–G);

● level 2 – GCSEs (grade A*–C);

● level 3 – A levels;

● level 4 – foundation degree;

- level 5 – degree;

- level 6 – honours degree;

- level 7 – masters degree;

- level 8 – Doctor of Philosophy (PhD).

Further information regarding qualifications and levels can be found at the direct.gov website via the internet shortcut http://tinyurl.com/66ftqx.

There are three teaching qualifications which fit into the new structure:

- Award in Preparing to Teach in the Lifelong Learning Sector (PTLLS) – a threshold licence to teach, with a credit value of six, at levels 3 and 4;

- Certificate in Teaching in the Lifelong Learning Sector (CTLLS) with a credit value of 24, at levels 3 and 4, for associate teachers;

- Diploma in Teaching in the Lifelong Learning Sector (DTLLS) with a credit value of 120, at level 5 and above, for full teachers.

If you are an *associate teacher*, you will need to take PTLLS and CTLLS. If you are a *full teacher* you will need to take PTLLS and DTLLS. All teachers must register with the Institute for Learning (IfL), the professional body for teachers, trainers, tutors and trainee teachers in the Learning and Skills Sector, and maintain their continuing professional development (CPD). Once registered, you must abide by their Code of Professional Practice; further details can be found via their website www.ifl.ac.uk.

For the purpose of the new teaching regulations, the IfL definitions of *associate* and *full* teacher apply whether you are working on a full time, part time, fractional, fixed term, temporary or agency basis:

> *Associate Teaching role means a teaching role that carries significantly less than the full range of teaching responsibilities and does not require the teacher to demonstrate an extensive range of knowledge, understanding and application of curriculum innovation or curriculum delivery strategies.*

> *Full Teaching role means a teaching role that carries the full range of teaching responsibilities and requires the teacher to demonstrate an extensive range of knowledge, understanding and application of curriculum innovation or curriculum delivery strategies.*
> Institute for Learning – www.ifl.ac.uk/services/p_wwv_page?id=340&session_id=

The Principles and Practice of Assessment unit can be taken independently from any of the teaching qualifications, as evidence towards CPD.

Registering with the IfL, gaining the relevant qualification, and maintaining your CPD, will enable you to apply for your teaching *status*. This will be either: Associate Teacher Learning and Skills (ATLS) for associate teachers, or Qualified Teacher Learning and Skills (QTLS) for full teachers. This is a requirement under the Further Education Teachers' Qualifications (England) Regulations (2007).

National Vocational Qualifications (NVQs) and the A1 and A2 Awards

National Vocational Qualifications (NVQs, or SVQs in Scotland) are work-related, competence-based qualifications which reflect the skills and knowledge needed for a person to do a job effectively.

NVQs are based on national occupational standards (NOS), which include statements of performance which describe what a competent person in a particular occupation is expected to be able to do. The standards are usually made up of performance criteria and knowledge requirements which a person must prove they can successfully meet. These form units of competence, which can be taken independently of one another and can be built up over time to achieve a full qualification. NVQs are usually assessed in the workplace by a qualified assessor; however, off the job training can also take place to help cover the knowledge requirements. The work of the assessor is quality assured by an internal verifier who samples their decisions, and an external verifier who will visit from an Awarding/Examining body.

A number of organisations are involved in the process of developing, delivering, awarding and ensuring the quality of NVQs.

- Sector Skills Councils (SSCs) are overseen by the Alliance of Sector Skills Councils (ASSC), and identify, define and update the standards of competence for particular occupations.

- Awarding/Examining bodies formulate the standards into qualifications. They then gain SSC endorsement prior to submission to the Qualifications and Curriculum Authority (QCA) for accreditation.

- QCA accredits the qualifications and monitors all Awarding/Examining bodies.

- Awarding/Examining bodies approve assessment centres, for example, colleges and training providers, who will assess and quality assure the NVQs.

- External verifiers from the Awarding/Examining body will monitor the centre's administration, assessment and quality assurance systems. The Awarding/Examining body will issue certificates to successful learners.

In Scotland, where the system of vocational education and training differs from that of the rest of Great Britain, the Scottish Qualifications Authority (SQA) accredits all Scottish Vocational Qualifications (SVQs).

Awarding/Examining bodies and centres must adhere to the QCA NVQ Code of Practice (2006). The Code aims to promote quality, consistency, accuracy and fairness in the assessment and awarding of all NVQs. The Code also contains *sanctions* which Awarding/Examining bodies can place upon approved centres if they do not meet the criteria contained within it.

Learners working towards an NVQ are often referred to as *candidates*; however, for consistency, the chapters in this book will refer to them as *learners*.

If you are an NVQ assessor within an approved centre, it is a requirement that you hold, or are working towards, either:

- Learning and Development Level 3: Unit A1 – *Assess Candidates Using a Range of Methods*, if you assess performance and knowledge, or

- Learning and Development Level 3: Unit A2 – *Assess Candidates' Performance through Observation*, if you observe performance in your learners' place of work.

These units have been available for several years, and will be updated in the near future to come in line with the QCF requirements. Whilst you are working towards your Award, your decisions will need to be countersigned by another qualified assessor in the same subject area. Appendix 2 contains the A1 and A2 standards.

Summary

In this chapter you have learnt about:

- the structure of the book and how to use it;

- Lifelong Learning professional teaching standards;

- National Vocational Qualifications (NVQs) and the A1 and A2 Awards.

References and further information

Gravells, A. (2008) *Preparing to Teach in the Lifelong Learning Sector* (3rd edn). Exeter: Learning Matters.

Gravells, A. and Simpson, S (2008) *Planning and Enabling Learning in the Lifelong Learning Sector.* Exeter: Learning Matters.

LLUK (2006) *New Overarching Professional Standards for Teachers, Tutors and Trainers in the Lifelong Learning Sector.* London: Skills for Business.

QCA (2006), *NVQ Code of Practice.* London: QCA.

Websites

Alliance of Sector Skills Councils – www.sscalliance.org

Further Education Teachers' Qualifications (England) Regulations (2007) – http://www.legislation.gov.uk/si/si2007/20072264.htm

Institute for Learning – www.ifl.ac.uk

Lifelong Learning UK – www.lluk.org.uk

Qualifications and Credit Framework – www.qca.org.uk/qca_8150.aspx

Qualifications and Curriculum Authority (QCA) – www.qca.org.uk

Scottish Qualifications Authority (SQA) – www.sqa.org.uk

Introduction

In this chapter you will learn about:

- concepts and principles of assessment;

- the assessment cycle;

- roles and responsibilities within the assessment process;

- communicating with others.

There are activities and examples to help you reflect on the above which will assist your understanding of the key concepts and principles of assessment.

Chapter 7 contains useful pro-formas you may wish to use.

This chapter contributes towards the following: scope (S), knowledge (K) and practice (P) aspects of the professional standards (A–F domains) for teachers, tutors and trainers in the Lifelong Learning Sector.

AS1, AS2, AS5;
AK1.1, AK4.1, AK5.1, AK5.2, AK6.1, AK6.2, AK7.1, AK7.2;
AP1.1, AP4.1, AP5.1, AP5.2, AP6.1, AP7.1;
BS1, BS2, BS3, BS4;
BK1.1, BK1.3, BK2.2, BK2.3, BK2.7, BK3.5, BK4.1;
BP1.3, BP2.7, BP3.1, BP3.5, BP4.1;
CS2;
CP1.1, CP2.1;
DK2.1;
ES1, ES2, ES3, ES5;
EK1.1, EK2.2, EK2.3, EK2.4, EK3.2, EK5.1, EK5.2, EK5.3;
EP2.2, EP2.4, EP5.1, EP5.5;
FS2;
FK2.1, FK4.2;
FP2.1, FP4.2.

This chapter contributes towards the following A1 and A2 standards:

A1.1c, A1.1d, A1.1f, A1.1g, A1.1h, A1.1i, A1.1k, A1.1l;
A1.2e, A1.2f, A1.3f;
A1.4a;
A2.1a, A2.1b, A2.1c, A2.1d, A2.1f, A2.1g;
A2.2c, A2.2d, A2.2h;
A2.3e;
A2.4d, A2.4e.

Concepts and principles of assessment

Assessment is a way of finding out if learning has taken place. It enables you, the assessor, to ascertain if your learner has gained the required skills and knowledge needed at a given point towards their programme or qualification. You may be teaching and assessing groups and/or individuals within your organisation, assessing online programmes, or assessing individuals in their place of work, for example towards a National Vocational Qualification (NVQ). Depending upon the subject you are assessing, you will need to devise suitable ways of assessing your learners to check their progress. It could be that assessment materials have already been produced for you, for example, assignments, written questions or tests.

A test is a systematic procedure for measuring a sample of a student's behaviour.
Reece, I. and Walker, S. (2007:44)

Tests can assess skills and knowledge, as well as behaviour. Having clear marking criteria, and sample answers, will help you make an informed assessment decision.

Assessment is a regular process; it might not be always be formalised, but you will be observing what your learners are doing, asking them questions, and reviewing their progress. If you also teach or train, your learners will be demonstrating their knowledge and skills regularly, for example through activities and tasks. You are therefore constantly making judgements about their progress, and how they could improve. You should also be aware of the impact that your comments, marks and grades can have on your learners' confidence. When giving feedback, try and be constructive; sometimes negative feedback can be constructive if given skilfully. Comments and feedback which specifically focus on the activity or work produced, rather than the individual, will be more helpful and motivating to your learners.

Assessments are usually:

- internally set – produced by you, or your organisation, for example, questions, projects or assignments, which will also be marked by you;

- externally set – usually by an Awarding/Examining body, for example, an examination at the end of the programme. These will be marked either by you, a colleague, or the Awarding/Examining body.

The starting point for devising or using assessments should be the programme syllabus or qualification handbook. This should state how the subject should be assessed, and will give information and guidance in the form of an *assessment strategy*. Standard Setting Bodies (SSB) or Sector Skills Councils (SSC) will provide information regarding the assessment strategy for a particular subject, which can usually be obtained via their website. The Qualifications and Curriculum Authority (QCA), Quality Assurance Agency (QAA) for Higher Education and each Awarding/Examining body will also have requirements regarding assessment which you should familiarise yourself with.

Activity

Obtain the programme syllabus or qualification handbook for the subject you will be assessing. This will usually be available from the relevant Awarding/Examining body website, or your organisation will probably have a copy. Have a look at the contents, and see what the assessment strategy states.

The purpose of the strategy is to ensure the subject is assessed in accordance with relevant guidance and regulations, to give a quality service to your learners, and maintain the reputation of your organisation and the qualification. The assessment strategy should state how the subject should be assessed, and subsequent results recorded. It should also state the experience, professional development and qualifications that assessors should hold. Quality assurance requirements, for example internal and external verification or moderation, will also be stated. Your organisation may also have an *assessment policy* which you should familiarise yourself with.

Following your organisation's policy and the relevant assessment strategy will ensure you are clear about the requirements as to how your subject should be assessed. You should not create any additional assessment criteria to those stated. However, you could create additional activities for your learners to carry out, based around the existing criteria. This would help you see how your learners are progressing prior to issuing any formal assessments.

The assessment cycle

Assessment cycle

Depending upon the subject you are assessing and whether it is academic (theory) or vocational (practical) you will usually follow the assessment cycle. The cycle will continue until all aspects of the qualification have been successfully achieved by your learner, or they decide to leave. Records must be maintained throughout to satisfy your organisation, the regulatory authorities and Awarding/Examining bodies.

- Initial assessment – ascertaining if your learner has any previous knowledge or experience of the subject or topic to be assessed. Relevant initial assessment activities will also give you information regarding your learners; for example any special assessment requirements they may have, their learning style, or any training they may need.

- Assessment planning – agreeing suitable types and methods of assessment with each learner, setting appropriate target dates, involving others as necessary – for example colleagues or workplace supervisors – and following relevant guidelines.

- Assessment activity – this could be assessor led: for example observation or questioning, or learner led: for example completing assignments or gathering appropriate evidence of competence. Records of what was assessed should always be maintained.

- Assessment decision and feedback – making a judgement of success or otherwise. Giving constructive feedback and agreeing any further action that may be necessary. An overall tracking sheet should be completed to enable you to clearly see what progress each learner has made towards each aspect of the qualification.

- Review of progress – the assessment plan can be reviewed and updated at any time until your learner completes their programme or qualification. Reviewing progress with your learners will give you an opportunity to discuss any other issues that may be relevant to their progress. Reviewing the assessment activities used will give you the opportunity to amend them if necessary.

The cycle will then begin again with an initial assessment regarding the next topic to be assessed. Throughout the cycle standardisation of assessment practice between assessors should take place; this will help ensure the consistency and fairness of decisions. Internal verification/moderation will also take place as part of the quality assurance process.

Activity

Find out what documents you need to use to support the assessment process at your organisation. Are they available in hard copy format, or do you need to download them from the computer system?

Always be prepared by having a few of the relevant documents available; you never know when you might need them quickly.

Assessment can take place in different environments depending upon what is being assessed and why. Some examples are:

- classroom – activities, tests, role-play, projects, presentations;

- hall – exams;

- library or home – assignments, research;

- outside environment – practical activities;

- workplace – observations and questions;

- workshop – practical tests.

Wherever you are assessing you will need to ensure both you and your learners are suitably prepared, and that you follow the assessment strategy and relevant guidelines.

Example

Cameron had planned to give his learners a test to check their progress so far, prior to moving onto the next topic. He had prepared a multiple choice test containing 30 questions to be completed within one hour. He decided to change the layout of the room from tables in groups to tables in rows. When the learners arrived, they were confused as to what was happening, some became stressed and upset when told they were to take a test. When Cameron marked the tests, most of the learners had not achieved the pass mark. After considering why, he realised he had been so focused on producing the test, he had forgotten to inform the learners about it. He had gone straight into the assessment activity part of the cycle without planning it with the learners first.

Assessment should focus on improving learning, whilst helping your learner achieve their qualification. It should help your learners realise how they are progressing, and what they need to do to improve.

Roles and responsibilities within the assessment process

Your responsibilities may include:

- attending meetings, exhibitions, award ceremonies, presentation events;

- carrying out assessments according to the Awarding/Examining body require-ments;

- checking the authenticity of any witness testimonies;

- completing and maintaining safe and secure records;

- countersigning other assessors' judgements;

- dealing with any appeals made against your assessment decisions;

- following organisational and regulatory body procedures;

- giving constructive and developmental feedback to your learners;

- identifying and dealing with any barriers to fair assessment;

- implementing internal and external verifier action points;

- liaising with others involved in the assessment process;

- making judgements towards the assessment criteria;

- maintaining occupational competence;

- negotiating and agreeing assessment plans;

- making best use of different assessment types and methods;

- providing statistics to managers;

- reviewing learner progress;

- standardising practice with other assessors;

- supporting learners with special assessment requirements, dealing with sensitive issues in a supportive manner;

- working towards relevant qualifications.

If you are unsure of any aspect of your assessor role or responsibilities, make sure you ask a colleague or your manager. You may be the only assessor for your particular subject within your organisation so it is therefore important that you liaise with your manager or internal verifier/moderator to ensure you are interpreting the subject or qualification requirements correctly. If you are a member of a team of assessors, you will need to ensure you all work together to give your learners equal and fair access to assessment opportunities. You will need to attend regular meetings, and work as a team to support the development and achievement of your learners.

The assessment process is a systematic procedure which should be followed to give your learner a positive experience, keep them motivated, and help them achieve their aim. During each phase of the assessment cycle, you will perform certain roles, and have responsibilities which should have been defined in your job description. You may be employed purely to assess learners, or you might also teach or train. If you don't have a specific job description for your assessor role from your organisation, the Awarding/Examining body will usually have guidance for you to follow.

Activity

Look at your job description; it might be part of your contract of employment. If you don't have one, look at the information contained in the Awarding/Examining body syllabus or handbook. Check that you feel confident at carrying out everything listed. If not, reading these should help, and you could talk to colleagues to see if they have any advice for you.

If you only assess, you might not consider yourself as a teacher or trainer, but you might find you are guiding, mentoring, coaching or supporting your learners informally in some way.

Example

Joan is assessing NVQ level 2 in Floristry. She visits each learner once a month in their place of work to observe their competence, and asks questions to check knowledge. Whilst carrying out an assessment with Ben, she realises he is not quite competent. Joan demonstrates how to perform one of the tasks expected and then Ben has a go. Joan asks Ben to practise this over the next few days, and then she will return the following month to carry out a formal assessment.

In this example, Joan has carried out a coaching session with Ben by demonstrating the task and then encouraging him to do it. If you are demonstrating something in front of a group of learners, always check if they are left or right handed as this could change the way they see things. When they look at you, your right hand will be on their left. If you are demonstrating on a one-to-one basis, try and stand or sit next to your learner rather than facing them.

NVQs are an excellent way for competent staff to demonstrate their skills and knowledge in their place of work, and to gain a qualification. However, if there are aspects of the qualification they are not familiar with, training will need to take place. This might occur with the *knowledge and understanding* requirements. If you issue a series of questions to test these, all the questions must be answered correctly. Questions to assess NVQs should not be marked with grades, for example, A, B, or C: they are either right or wrong. If a question is not answered correctly, then the learner will need to redo it. An initial assessment for each unit would greatly help identify what may need to be learnt first, before any assessment takes place. If you are not familiar with how to teach or train, you can take a relevant qualification.

As an assessor, you will need to follow various regulations: for example, the Health and Safety at Work Act (1974). This places a legal responsibility upon you, as well as your organisation and your learners. If you see a potential hazard, you must do something about this before an accident occurs.

Activity

Locate the Health and Safety policy within your organisation, read it to check you understand the contents, and find out who you would need to go to if you had any problems or queries. If you are assessing outside your organisation, make sure you know the details of what you should do if a problem occurs.

You might also have to carry out a *risk assessment* to ensure the assessment activity and area are safe for all concerned. This is a requirement under the Management of Health and Safety at Work Regulations (1999), and can normally be achieved by a *walk through* of the area, and a discussion with those involved. However, a formal record must be kept in case of any incidents. You probably unconsciously carry out a risk assessment whenever you do anything; for example, when crossing the road, you would automatically check the traffic flow before stepping out. The health and safety of yourself, your colleagues and your learners is of paramount importance. The Health and Safety Executive has produced a useful leaflet which can be accessed at: www.hse.gov.uk/services/education/information.htm.

You will need to follow your organisation's policies and procedures, which will include:

- access and fair assessment;
- appeals and complaints;
- copyright and data protection;
- equal opportunities;
- equality and diversity;
- health and safety.

When you commenced your job role, you should have been given information regarding these. If not, make sure you are familiar with them.

Your role as an assessor will also be to inspire and motivate your learners. If you are enthusiastic and passionate about your subject, this will help to stimulate and challenge your learners. Your learners may already be motivated for personal reasons and be enthusiastic and want to perform well. This is known as *intrinsic motivation*. Your learners may be motivated by a need to learn, for example to gain a qualification, promotion or pay rise at work, known as *extrinsic motivation*. If you can recognise the difference between your learners' *wants* and *needs*, you can see why they are motivated and ensure you make their experience meaningful and relevant. Whatever type of motivation your learners have will be transformed, for better or worse, by what happens during their assessment experience. Some learners may lack self-confidence, or have previous experiences of assessment that were not very positive. Many factors can affect your learners' motivation; therefore you need to ensure you treat all your learners as individuals, using their names, and making the assessment experience interesting and meaningful. Some learners may need more attention than others. Just because one learner is progressing well doesn't mean you can focus on those that aren't; all your learners need encouragement and feedback. You may not be able to change the environment or the resources you are using, but remaining professional and making the best of what you have will help encourage your learners' development.

Example

Frank has a group of learners working towards a GCSE in Geography. One of his learners, Rea, seems to be losing motivation and is not paying attention during sessions. As Frank knows she enjoys working with computers, he arranges for the class to move to the computer workshop to use the BBC 16+ website, which has activities and tests for learners to complete. These will give immediate scores which will help Frank monitor his learners' progress, and retain the motivation of Rea and the group.

You need to encourage your learners to reach their maximum potential. If you use assessment activities which are too difficult, learners may struggle and become frustrated and anxious. If assessments are too easy, learners may become bored. Knowing your learners and differentiating for their needs will help their motivation.

If you have learners who are quite motivated already, keep this motivation alive with regular challenges, and constructive and positive feedback. A lack of motivation can lead to disruption and apathy. If you are teaching or training as well as assessing, ensure you are reaching the different learning styles of your learners. It might be part of your responsibility to test your learners for their preferred style of learning. A learning styles test could be carried out as part of the initial assessment process. Fleming (1987) categorised learning styles as *visual, aural, read/write* and *kinaesthetic,* often referred to as VARK.

Activity

Carry out a search via the internet for learning styles, or ask in your organisation which learning styles tests they recommend. Compare different theorists and styles, some tests are more complex than others. Fleming's is available at www.vark-learn.com.

Knowing what style your learners are will help you plan suitable assessment activities. You might not be able to change the *formal* assessments required as part of the programme or qualification, but you might be able to devise *informal* assessments to suit your learners.

Example

Susan had always assessed her learners by assignments and tests. After encouraging them to take a learning styles test, she realised several of her learners are kinaesthetic. She has therefore changed some of her assessments to include role play and more practical activities.

Using assessment methods which cover all learning styles will ensure you are being inclusive, and make the activities more interesting to your learners.

As an assessor, you may not be the only person involved in the assessment process; there is of course your learner, and there may be others such as:

● administrators;

● countersignatories;

● different assessors;

● different markers;

● expert witnesses;

● examination officers;

- independent assessors;

- internal and external verifiers and moderators;

- mentors;

- invigilators;

- teachers, tutors and trainers.

You will need to liaise with anyone else involved in the assessment process, and communicate in a professional manner. You might have to plan for examinations to take place, in which case you will need to ensure the administration staff are aware of what will take place and when, as invigilators may be needed, and specific rooms timetabled accordingly.

If you are assessing learners in their place of work, it is best to plan ahead to arrange your visits according to location, for example, assessing learners in close proximity to ease the time and cost spent travelling. When assessing in the work-place, notify your learners' employers in advance, in case there is any reason they can't accommodate you on a particular day.

Where there are different markers or assessors involved with the same qualification, or even the same group of learners, you will need to meet to discuss how you have reached your decisions, and compare the marks given. You might *double mark* one another's work to ensure you are all being consistent. Prior to any assessments taking place, you would all need to ensure you have interpreted the assessment requirements and any marking schemes correctly.

Some of your learners might use a witness testimony as part of their evidence. This will usually come from someone who is an expert at the subject, and knows your learner. They will write a statement of how your learner has met the required outcomes; however, you will need to liaise with them to confirm the authenticity of the statement. All witnesses should sign a declaration, which is usually supplied by the Awarding/ Examining body, and they may require a copy of the witness's certificates and curriculum vitae. If witnesses are involved, they will need to be briefed as to what they are expected to do, and should be familiar with the qualification being assessed.

You might teach a particular subject, but not assess it; for example, your learners may take an exam which is marked by the Awarding/Examining body, or a test which is marked by a colleague. If you assess an NVQ, some qualifications require an aspect of it, or a full unit, to be assessed by a different assessor. This process is known as *independent assessment* and is a QCA requirement for some qualifications. It allows for objectivity within the assessment process.

If your subject or qualification is quality assured, your internal and external verifiers/ moderators will sample your work to ensure your judgements are correct and fair.

Some learners might have a mentor, someone who is supporting and encouraging them whilst they go through the learning and assessment process. They may also have other teachers, trainers and tutors who are involved with their progress. However, do be aware of any sensitive or confidential issues relating to your learners which they may not wish you to pass on.

As an assessor, you will have professional boundaries within which to work. You will need to know what these are at your organisation, and not overstep them. Boundaries are about knowing where your role as an assessor stops. You may have a learner who needs more support than others; you would not be helping them if you did their work for them. You would be better pointing them to where they could find things out for themselves, giving them autonomy in the learning and assessment process. You may have some learners who have personal problems and not feel confident at giving them advice. Knowing whom to refer them to would ensure they receive expert information.

Communicating with others

You will need to communicate with other people who are involved in the assessment process of your learners. You should remain professional at all times you are representing your organisation and although people may not always remember your name, you may be known as *that person from XYZ organisation*. You therefore need to create a good and lasting impression of yourself and your organisation. You may have to deal with inspectors and auditors from the various stakeholders involved with your programme or qualification. They will need to satisfy themselves that you are capable of assessing the programme or qualification correctly.

People you may need to communicate with, besides your learners, include those internal to your organisation, for example:

- colleagues;

- internal verifiers/moderators;

- managers;

- mentors;

- support staff.

You may also need to liaise with people who are external to your organisation, for example:

- employers;

- external verifiers/moderators;

- funding body staff;

- inspectors;

- parents, guardians, or carers;

- regulatory body staff;

- staff at training events and exhibitions, etc;

- staff from other organisations and agencies;

- witnesses and others involved in the assessment of your learners.

You may act differently depending upon the circumstances. For example informally with colleagues, but formally with managers and employers. Communication can be verbal, non-verbal, or written. Whichever method you use, communication is a means of passing on information from one person to another.

Skills of communicating effectively include the way you speak, listen and express yourself, for example with body language. You need to be confident and organised with what you wish to convey; the way you do this will give an impression of yourself. You may have to attend meetings or video conferences, and wherever you are with other people, they will make assumptions about you based on what they see and hear. You may have to write reports, memos or e-mails; the way you express yourself when writing is as important as when speaking.

You will not have a second chance to make a first impression, therefore it is important to portray yourself in a professional way, not only with what you say, but in the way you say it, your attitude, body language and dress. A warm and confident smile, positive attitude, self assurance and the use of eye contact will all help when communicating, particularly if you are meeting someone for the first time.

Activity

Find out who you need to communicate with, either internally or externally, regarding the subjects you are assessing. If you are ever unsure of anything, don't be afraid to ask someone.

It could be that you need to write reports of progress for parents or guardians. If you have learners who are attending a programme in conjunction with a school you may need to liaise with their staff. You may need to communicate with employers or managers/supervisors whose staff you are assessing. If this is the case, make sure you are aware of any protocols involved, and follow your organisation's procedures.

When communicating verbally, your tone, pace and inflections are all important factors in getting your message across. If you speak too quickly or softly, others may not hear everything you say; always try to speak clearly. It is useful to consider what reactions you want to achieve from the information you are communicating, and if others react differently, you will need to amend your methods. You may be communicating via the telephone, therefore unable to see any reactions to your words, which could lead to a misunderstanding. Always ask questions to check that the person you are communicating with has understood what you have said.

Non-verbal communication includes your body language and posture, for example gestures, and the way you stand or sit. Be conscious of your mannerisms, for example folded arms, hands in pockets, or the gestures you make, etc, and use eye contact with the person you are communicating with. The things you *don't* say are as important as those you *do* say.

Written communication, for example in the form of feedback for assessed work, or an e-mail, is also an expression of you. The way you convey your words and phrases, and your intention, may not be how it is read or understood by the other person. If you are working with learners via an online programme, you may never see them, but will probably build up a visual image; they may therefore be doing the same of you. Information can be easily misinterpreted; therefore the sender has to be sure the receiver will interpret any communication in the way that it was intended. You need to get your message across effectively; otherwise what you are conveying may not necessarily reflect your own thoughts and may cause a break-down in communication. Any written text cannot be taken back, so there is less room for errors or mistakes and you need to be clear about the exact meaning you wish to convey. Your writing style, words and syntax need checking for spelling, grammar and punctuation. Don't rely on a computer to check these, as it will not always realise the context in which you are writing. This is particularly the case when writing feedback to learners; if you make a spelling mistake, they will think it is correct as you are the more knowledgeable person.

You might give feedback to your learners via a computer: for example an e-mail or an e-assessment program. If you use this type of medium for communication and/or assessment purposes, try not to get in the habit of abbreviating words or cutting out vowels. It is important to express yourself in a professional way, other-wise misunderstanding and confusion may arise. Just imagine you are talking to the other person, and type your message appropriately.

Example

Aasif has a good professional working relationship with his group. He needs to e-mail his learners to remind them the room they will be in next week is to be changed due to examinations taking place in their usual room. He keeps his e-mail brief and to the point by stating 'Hi all, just a quick reminder that we will be in room G3 next week instead of G5, Aasif'. A bad alternative could have been: 'Hey, I told u last week we wld be in a different room cos of exams, so don't forget where u have to go, and dont get lost, A'.

The latter is unprofessional, is rather negative, contains errors, and doesn't convey where the learners should go. This would not give a good impression, and the learners may lose some respect for Aasif.

You may need to liaise with support staff within your organisation, perhaps to arrange help with preparing assessment materials and resources, or by making modifications or adaptations to equipment and materials. Some of your learners may need extra support with literacy or numeracy; if this is arranged make sure you check on their progress. You might also need to get in touch with others who have an involvement with your learners, for example, careers advisers, probation officers or social workers. If this is the case remember aspects of confidentiality, and keep notes of all discussions in case you need to refer to them again.

You might have learners who have excelled in some way, and your organisation or Awarding/Examining body may have an award or medal they could be nominated for. Your own organisation or department could hold a celebration event to pres-ent certificates to successful learners. This is also a way of obtaining positive publicity for your organisation.

Knowing who you need to deal with, how you should proceed, and what is involved in the assessment process should make your role as an assessor more rewarding and professional.

Summary

In this chapter you have learnt about:

- concepts and principles of assessment;

- the assessment cycle;

- roles and responsibilities within the assessment process;

- communicating with others.

References and further information

QAA (2006), *Code of Practice for the Assurance of Academic Quality and Standards in Higher Education.* Gloucester: Quality Assurance Agency.

Health and Safety Executive (1999) *Management of Health and Safety at*

Work Regulations – Approved Code of Practice and Guidance (2nd edn). L21: HSE Books.

QCA (2006) *NVQ Code of Practice.* London: QCA.

Reece, I. and Walker, S. (2007) *Teaching, Training and Learning* (6th edn). Sunderland: Business Education Publishers Ltd.

Websites

14–19 Diplomas – www.dfes.gov.uk

BBC – www.bbc.co.uk/schools/websites/16/

Fleming's Learning Styles – www.vark-learn.com

Health and Safety Executive – www.hse.gov.uk

Office Safety & Risk Assessments – www.officesafety.co.uk

Quality Assurance Agency – www.qaa.ac.uk

Qualifications and Curriculum Authority – www.qca.org.uk

2 TYPES OF ASSESSMENT

Introduction

> In this chapter you will learn about:
>
> - types of assessment;
> - assessment planning.

There are activities and examples to help you reflect on the above which will assist your understanding of different types of assessment and how to plan for assessment.

Chapter 7 contains useful pro-formas you may wish to use.

This chapter contributes towards the following: scope (S), knowledge (K) and practice (P) aspects of the professional standards (A–F domains) for teachers, tutors and trainers in the Lifelong Learning Sector.

AS6;
AK1.1, AK2.1, AK3.1, AK4.1, AK5.1, AK5.2, AK6.1, AK6.2, AK7.1, AK7.3;
AP1.1, AP2.1, AP2.2, AP3.1, AP4.1, AP5.1, AP5.2, AP6.1, AP6.2, AP7.1, AP7.3;
BS1, BS2, BS3, BS4, BS5;
BK1.1, BK1.2, BK1.3, BK2.2, BK3.4, BK3.5, BK4.1, BK5.2;
BP1.1, BP1.2, BP1.3, BP2.1, BP2.2, BP2.3, BP3.5, BP4.1, BP5.1, BP5.2;
CS2, CS3, CK3.2, CK3.3, CK3.5;
CP2.1, CP3.2, CP3.3, CP3.5, CP4.2;
DS1, DS2, DS3;
DK1.1, DK2.1, DK2.2;
DP1.1, DP1.3, DP2.1, DP2.2;
ES1, ES2, ES3, ES5;
EK1.1, EK1.2, EK2.1, EK2.2, EK2.3, EK3.1, EK3.2, EK5.1, EK5.2, EK5.3;
EP1.2, EP2.1, EP2.2, EP2.4, EP3.1, EP3.2;
FS1, FS2;
FK1.1, FK1.2, FK2.1, FK4.1, FK4.2;
FP1.1, FP1.2, FP2.1, FP4.1, FP4.2.

This chapter contributes towards the following A1 and A2 standards:

A1.1a, A1.1b, A1.1c, A1.1d, A1.1e, A1.1f; A1.1g, A1.1h, A1.1i, A1.1k, A1.1l, A1.1m;
A1.2e, A1.2f, A1.3f;
A1.4a.

A2.1a, A2.1c, A2.1d, A2.1f, A2.1g;
A2.2a;
A2.3c;
A2.4d.

Types of assessment

Assessment gives a measure of learning at a given point in time. Relevant skills, knowledge and/or attitudes can be measured towards a subject or qualification. There are many different assessment methods, including tests, exams, assignments, observation, etc. There are also different types of assessment. These will usually be stated in the syllabus, and a useful reference table can be found at the end of this section. You may be familiar with some types such as initial (at the beginning), formative (ongoing) and summative (at the end). You may not be as familiar with other terms such as ipsative, norm, or criterion referencing. This section will explore various types of assessment to enable you to make relevant choices should you need to use a particular type.

Subjects that don't lead to a formal certificate are known as non-accredited; if a subject is accredited, it is through an Awarding or Examining body and a certificate will be issued. They will monitor the delivery and assessment of the qualification to ensure all their guidelines are being followed.

Prior to assessing your learners' progress towards their chosen subject, you need to carry out an *initial assessment* or *training needs analysis* to ascertain their skills and knowledge so far. These will include specific activities relating to the subject or qualification your learners will be taking. The results of these will help you plan what needs to be learnt and assessed, and can also trigger the process of accrediting prior experience and learning (APEL).

Example

Sharron has completed an initial assessment which was designed to evaluate her knowledge and skills towards the NVQ in Travel and Tourism. Sharron had started the NVQ at another organisation prior to moving to the area. Her assessor was able to see that she had already been assessed for three units fairly recently. Sharron was therefore accredited with these units once her assessor had confirmed all the requirements had been met. She therefore did not need to be reassessed.

You might also carry out a diagnostic assessment to see if your learners require any support with aspects such as literacy and numeracy.

Initial assessment will help to:

- agree an appropriate individual learning plan or assessment plan, with suitable targets;

- allow for differentiation and individual requirements to be met;

- ensure learners are on the right type of programme;

- ensure learners are taking the right programme at the right level;

- identify an appropriate starting point for each learner;

- identify any information which needs to be shared with colleagues;

- identify any specific additional support needs;

- identify learners' previous experience and achievements, using it as a foundation for further learning and assessment;

- identify learning styles;

- identify specific requirements, for example, the functional skills of maths, English and information and communication technology (ICT);

- inspire and motivate learners;

- involve learners, giving them confidence to agree targets.

Activity

Find out what initial and diagnostic assessments are used at your organisation. Will it be your responsibility to administer these, or is there a specialist person to do this?

There are lots of initial assessment materials available online. If you get the opportunity, carry out a search for *initial assessment* or *diagnostic assessment*.

The starting point for planning your assessment will be the syllabus. However, the subject or qualification you are assessing might not have a syllabus, or it could be called something else, such as:

- course outline;

- course specification;

- qualification handbook;

- programme guidelines;

- set of standards.

Most syllabi can be obtained directly from the Awarding/Examining body via their website. However, if you are assessing a non-accredited programme, you may be working from a syllabus produced by your organisation, or you may even have to write your own. The language used within the syllabus to denote what will need to be taught and assessed will usually be written as one of the following:

- ability outcomes;

- aims and objectives;

- assessment criteria;

- evidence requirements;

- learning outcomes;

- performance criteria;

- standards;

- statements of competence.

Activity

Look at the syllabus for your subject area; see how it is broken down into topics, which will have details of how each should be assessed. Does the syllabus give you guidance as to which assessment types and methods to use?

Different subjects will require different types of assessment, which can be carried out *formally* or *informally* depending upon the requirements. Formal assessments are usually planned and carried out according to the assessment criteria, whereas informal assessments can occur at any time, to check ongoing progress.

Example

Julie has been teaching French for Beginners which is assessed formally at the end of the programme. She will give her learners the written exam, and afterwards ask oral questions on an individual basis. The exam papers will be externally marked. Julie will be making the decision as to a pass or fail for the oral questions, depending upon the learners' responses. As Julie has taught the learners, and is assessing them too, a recording will be made of the oral questions and responses, in case of any appeal by her learners.

In this example, the exam and oral questions are provided by the Awarding/ Examining body and are therefore a *formal* assessment type. Julie will not mark the exam, but will make the decision regarding responses to the oral questions. Guidance has been given for suggested answers, which will ensure Julie remains *objective* when making her decision. If answers had not been supplied, she could find herself being *subjective* – being biased towards a particular learner if they hadn't quite answered the question correctly. Throughout the programme, Julie has been asking questions, and using quizzes and discussions to informally assess her learners' ongoing progress.

Assessment *types* are different to assessment *methods*. A method is *how* the assessment type will be used.

Formal assessment methods can include:

- assignments;

- essays;

- exams;

- observations;

- multiple choice questions;

- tests.

Informal assessment methods can include:

- discussions;

- gapped handouts (cloze sentence/missing words);

- journals/diaries;

- peer feedback;

- puzzles and quizzes;

- role play.

All these methods and more are explored further in Chapter 3. All assessment methods and types should be suitable to the level of your learners. A level 1 learner might struggle to maintain a journal of their progress and a level 2 learner may not be mature enough to accept peer feedback. A level 3 learner may feel a puzzle is too easy, and so on. Some learners may respond better to informal formative assessment rather than formal summative assessment. You need to consider the assessment requirement for your subject, and how you can best implement these, without changing the assessment criteria.

Example

Maria sees her group of learners once a week for an Art and Design programme. Each week, she commences the session by asking some questions regarding the topics covered in the previous week. This is informal formative assessment to ensure her learners have understood the topics taught. At the end of term, she will give a formal summative assignment, which will test their skills and knowledge.

Questions are a really useful type of formative assessment, to ensure your learners are acquiring the necessary knowledge before moving onto a new topic. They can also be useful as a type of summative assessment at the end of a programme.

When planning which assessment type to use, you need to ensure it will be *valid* and *reliable*, and that you are being *fair* and *ethical* with all your decisions.

- Valid – the assessment type is appropriate to the subject/qualification being assessed.

- Reliable – if the assessment is carried out again with similar learners, similar results will be achieved.

- Fair – the assessment type is appropriate to all your learners at the required level, is inclusive, i.e. available to all, and differentiates for any particular needs.

- Ethical – the assessment takes into account confidentiality, integrity, safety and security.

These aspects must always be considered carefully to ensure you are only assessing what is necessary and relevant, at a level to suit your learners, and that there is no chance of favouritism occurring with assessment decisions.

The style of qualification you assess will also determine the assessment type used, for example an academic programme could be *summatively* assessed by an exam, whereas a vocational programme could be *formatively* assessed by observation and questioning.

Activity

Decide upon the types of assessment you will use for your subject. How will you ensure they are valid, reliable, fair and ethical? Are they appropriate for the levels of your learners? Look at the table on pages 28–30 for ideas.

You might have all the details of assessment types and methods provided for you; if not, you will need to carefully select these to suit your subject, the situation and your learners. You might decide to assess your learners on a formative basis throughout their time with you, with a summative test at the end. This would enable you to see how they are progressing, and whether they will be ready or not prior to taking the final test. You might be provided with assignments for your learners to complete at set times during the programme. To be sure your learners are ready you could use activities, quizzes and tasks for your learners to carry out prior to the assignments. This would make the assessment process more interesting, and highlight any areas which need further development. If you are assessing a programme whereby the activities are provided for you, for example tests or exams, there is often the tendency to teach purely what is required to achieve a pass. Learners may therefore not gain valuable additional skills and knowledge. Teaching to pass tests does not maximise learners' ability and potential.

Bloom (1956) believed that education should focus on the *mastery* of subjects and the promotion of higher forms of thinking, rather than an approach which simply transfers facts. Bloom's Taxonomy (1956) model attempts to classify all learning into three *overlapping domains*:

1 *cognitive domain* (intellectual capability, i.e. *knowledge* or *thinking*);

2 *affective domain* (feelings, emotions and behaviour, i.e. *attitudes* or *beliefs*);

3 *psychomotor domain* (manual and physical skills, i.e. *skills* or *actions*).

The three domains are summarised as knowledge, attitudes and skills, or *think, feel, do*. Your learners should benefit from the development of knowledge and intellect (*cognitive domain*); attitudes and beliefs (*affective domain*); and the ability to put physical skills into effect (*psychomotor domain*). You would therefore assess your learners at the right level for their learning, at the appropriate time. Each domain contains *objectives* at different levels, such as, list, describe, explain, and analyse.

Example

Pierre has a group of level 1 learners working towards a Certificate in Welding Skills. He carries out formative assessment of his learners using objectives such as list and state (to test knowledge), adopt and familiarise (to test attitudes), and attempt and use (to test skills). When he is sure his learners have mastered the topics, he will give them a summative test which will cover the required knowledge, attitudes and skills needed to achieve the certificate.

If Pierre used objectives such as *explain, justify* and *facilitate*, these would be too high a level for his learners. If his learners progress to level 2 and 3, Pierre would then use higher level objectives. A comprehensive list of objectives at different levels can be found in the companion book by Gravells and Simpson (2008) *Planning and Enabling Learning in the Lifelong Learning Sector.*

Your job role might be to assess a National Vocational Qualification (NVQ); you might not carry out any formal teaching prior to assessing, but will guide and support your learner to ensure they are ready. NVQs are based upon what your learner *can do* and they need to prove this to you by producing *evidence* of their skills and knowledge. This evidence is often produced as a *portfolio,* i.e. in a ring binder, or by *electronic* means, i.e. all the evidence and assessment records are saved to a computer. Assessment is usually in your learner's place of work and they might not attend any formal training sessions. As there is no exam, quality assurance will take place by an *internal verifier* who will sample your assessment decisions. The internal verifier works for the same organisation as the assessor, and their decisions will subsequently be sampled by the external verifier from the relevant Awarding/Examining body. NVQs allow learners to work at their own pace and be assessed when they are ready.

NVQs are usually made up of *units,* a particular work role or function within the qualification. The units contain *elements,* which are the activities required to perform the work role, and *performance criteria,* which are the processes involved. There may also be *range statements* or *scope* which are the different contexts within which your learner must demonstrate competence. Evidence requirements might be listed for each unit, to ensure everything is met. There are also statements of required *knowledge and understanding* which must also be achieved. The latter are often implicit within the evidence provided, or can be assessed by the use of written or oral questions.

Example

Abdul is taking the NVQ in Customer Service at level 2. He is currently working towards unit 5: Provide customer service within the rules. It has two elements, each containing four performance criteria, and there are eight knowledge and understanding requirements. Abdul will need to provide evidence that he can meet all of these whilst at work. The evidence requirements clearly state what should be provided. Both Abdul and his assessor are therefore very clear about what needs to be carried out. Assessment of his qualification will be ongoing, i.e. formative, until he has completed all the units.

Besides NVQs, there are vocational qualifications and academic qualifications. Vocational qualifications are often written in a style similar to NVQs, but they don't need to be assessed in the workplace; simulation can take place, or they can be assessed in a realistic working environment (RWE), for example a motor vehicle workshop within a training centre. Academic qualifications are usually based on theory, and assessed by formal methods such as an exam, test or series of assignments. The assignments might be provided by the Awarding/Examining body, or you may have to write them yourself.

If there are no clear guidelines for assessment, you might find yourself being *subjective* rather than *objective*. That is, you make your own decision without reference to any criteria.

Activity

Ask a colleague, friend or family member to make a paper plane, and tell them you will assess them whilst they are doing this. Once they have made it, ask them to fly it and give them a grade of pass, refer or fail.

How did they do and what helped you make your decision? Was it a pass because they made the plane and it flew for a few seconds? Was it a referral because they made the plane but it didn't fly, or was it a fail because they didn't know how to make a paper plane, you just assumed they could? Without any criteria to assess against, you will be making a *subjective* decision, which could be wrong. Producing assessment criteria will ensure your assessment is valid and reliable, and you are being fair and ethical.

If you have a group of learners whom you are testing, for example, using written questions to check their knowledge which may be graded, i.e. A–E, you will need to produce expected responses to ensure you are being fair when marking. If you don't you might find yourself subconsciously giving a higher mark to the best learners in your group. You should always remain objective when assessing, not have any favourite learners, and follow the marking criteria correctly. Otherwise, you may find your learners may appeal against your decision.

If you want to compare the achievements of your group against one another, you could use *norm-referencing*. This would proportion your marks accordingly, as there will always be those in your group who will achieve a high mark, those who will achieve a low mark, leaving the rest in the middle. You would allocate your marks according to a quota, for example, the top 20% would achieve an A, the next 20% a B, and so on. Norm referencing uses the achievement of a group to set the standards for specific grades, or for how many learners will pass or fail. This type of assessment is useful to maintain consistency of results over time; whether the test questions are easy or hard, there will always be those achieving a high grade or a lower grade, whatever their marks.

Example

Petra has a group of 25 learners who have just taken a test consisting of 20 questions – she wants to allocate grades A–E to her group. She has worked out the top 20% will achieve an A, the second 20% a B and so on. When she marks the tests, she is surprised to see the lowest mark was 16 out of 20, meaning a grade E. Even though the learner had done well in the test, they were still given a low grade in comparison with the rest of the group.

A fairer method of marking would have been to set a pass mark, for example, 15. Learners achieving 14 or below could be referred and retake the test at a later date.

Criterion referencing enables learners to achieve based upon their own merit, as their achievements are not compared with one another. All learners therefore have equality of opportunity. If grades are allocated, for example a distinction, credit or pass, there will be specific criteria which must have been met for each. Either these criteria will be supplied by the Awarding/Examining body, or you may need to produce them yourself.

Example

Pass – described the activity.

Credit – described and analysed the activity.

Distinction – described, analysed and critically reflected upon the activity.

The following table summarises various types of assessment.

Academic	Assessment of theory or knowledge.
Aptitude	A diagnostic test to assess your learner's ability for a particular vocation.
Assessor led	Assessment is planned and carried out by the assessor, for example an observation.
Benchmarking	A way of evaluating learner performance against an accepted standard. Once a standard is set, it can be used as a basis for the expectation of achievements within other groups/learners.
Competence based	*Can do* statements that learners need to perform, for example NVQ performance criteria.
Criterion referencing	Assessing what your learner *must achieve* to meet a certain standard.
Diagnostic	A specific assessment relating to a particular topic or subject and level, which builds on initial assessment. Sometimes called a *skills scan*. The results determine what needs to be learnt or assessed in order to progress further. Some types of diagnostic assessments can also identify learners with dyslexia, dyspraxia, dysgraphia, dyscalculia, etc.

Direct	Evidence provided by your learner towards their qualification, for example work products.
Evidence	Assessment is based upon items your learner provides to prove their competence.
External	Assessments set and marked externally by the relevant Awarding/Examining body.
Formal	Assessment which involves the recognition and recording of achievement.
Formative	Ongoing, interim or continuous assessment. Can be used to assess skills and/or knowledge in a progressive way, to build on topics learnt and plan future learning and assessments. Often referred to as assessment *for* learning, allowing further learning to take place prior to more assessments.
Holistic	Assessing several aspects of a qualification at the same time.
Independent	An aspect of the qualification is assessed by someone who has not been involved with your learner for any other part of their training or assessment.
Indirect	Evidence provided by others regarding your learner's progress, for example a witness testimony from a workplace supervisor.
Informal	Assessment can take place, for example, questioning during a review of progress with your learner, or an observation during a group activity.
Initial	Assessment at the beginning of a programme or unit, relating to the subject being learnt and assessed, to identify your learner's starting point and level. Initial assessment can also include learning styles tests, and literacy, numeracy and ICT tests. The latter can be used as a basis to help and support learners.
Integrated	Information acquired in a learning context is put into practice and assessed in your learner's workplace.
Internal	Assessments carried out within an organisation, either internally set and marked, or externally set by the relevant Awarding/Examining body and internally marked.
Ipsative	A process of self-assessment. Learners match their own achievements against a set of standards, or keep a reflective journal of their learning so far. This is useful for learners to see their own progress and development; however, they do need to work autonomously and be honest about their achievements.
Learner led	Learners produce evidence, or let their assessor know when they are ready to be assessed.
Norm referencing	Comparing the results of learner achievements with one another, for example setting a pass mark to enable a certain percentage of a group to achieve or not.
Objective	An assessment decision which is based around the criteria being assessed, not a personal opinion or decision.
Proficiency	An assessment to test ability, for example, riding a bike.

Process	The assessment of routine skills or techniques is assessed, for example, to ensure your learner is following a set procedure. or Additional learning will take place besides that stated to achieve the assessment criteria.
Product	The outcome is assessed, not the process. For example a painting or a working model. or Teaching only the minimum amount required to pass an assessment.
Profiling	A way of recording learner achievements for each individual aspect of an assessment. Checklists can be a useful way to evidence these. More than one assessor can be involved in the process.
Qualitative	Assessment is based upon individual responses to open questions given to your learners. Clear criteria must be stated for the assessor to make a decision, as questions can be vague or misinterpreted.
Quantitative	Assessment is based upon *yes/no* or *true/false* responses, *agree/disagree* statements, or multiple choice tests, giving a clear right or wrong answer. Totals can be added to give results, for example 8 out of 10. Learners could pass purely by guessing the correct answers.
Screening	An informal process to assess if your learner has a language, literacy or numeracy skills need.
Subjective	A personal decision by the assessor, where the assessment criteria may not be clearly stated. This can be unfair to your learner.
Summative	Assessment at the end of a programme or unit, for example, an exam. If your learner does not pass, they will usually have the opportunity to retake. Often known as assessment *of* learning, as it shows what has been achieved from the learning process.
Triangulation	Using more than one assessment method, for example, observation, oral questioning and a test. This helps ensure the reliability and authenticity of your learner's work and makes the assessment process more interesting.
Vocational	Job related practical assessment, usually in your learner's place of work.

Assessment planning

Failing to plan how you are going to assess your learners may result in your learners failing the assessment activity. Assessment should be a two way process between you and your learners; you need to plan what you are going to do, and they need to know what is expected of them.

The way you plan to assess your learners will depend upon the:

● assessment method;

● assessment type;

- dates and times;
- environment;
- learners;
- level;
- organisational budget;
- resources;
- special requirements;
- staff;
- subject or qualification.

If you are assessing a subject with all the information and materials provided by the Awarding/Examining body, the process of planning will be quite straightforward.

Example

Harry has taught a numeracy programme, according to the syllabus, over three terms. At the end of each term, a summative test provided by the Awarding/Examining body is given to the learners, which Harry will invigilate and mark. A marking scheme has been provided for him. To plan for this, Harry ensured he had delivered all the required content within the time, arranged for the classroom to be formally laid out with desks in rows, and forewarned his group of the date and time of the test. Prior to this he gave them a formative test to check their progress. He ensured he had a clock on the wall and followed the invigilation guidelines.

Even though all the materials might be provided for you, you will still need to carry out some form of assessment planning, and inform your learners when assessment will take place. If you prepare a scheme of work, you will need to ensure time is planned for the relevant assessments, along with time for feedback. If your learners are working towards a formal qualification, you will need to ensure they have been registered with the appropriate Awarding/Examining body. It might not be your responsibility to carry out this task, but you should communicate the details of your learners to relevant staff. If a *record of attendance* or an *in-house certificate* will be issued to your learners, this information should be communicated to the person who will produce them. You will also need to inform your learners when they can expect to receive any feedback or formal recognition of their achievements. You also need to discuss what they can do if they disagree with the assessment planning process, such as whom they could go to if they couldn't resolve a situation. Completing an *assessment plan* and *review record* will formalise the process; an example is available in Chapter 7.

You might assess on an individual basis within your organisation, or at your learner's place of work. Or you might assess group work such as role-play or discussions in a classroom. If it is the latter, you would need to assess each individual's contribution towards the assessment requirements. Otherwise you would be passing the whole group, when some may not have contributed much at all. If you are related to, or know personally, the learners you will assess, you should notify your organisation of any conflict of interest. They may also need to notify the relevant Awarding/Examining body, in case you are not allowed to assess a learner if they are a direct member of your family, or your spouse's family.

Assessment planning should be specific, measurable, achievable, realistic and time bound (SMART).

- Specific – the task relates only to the standards/learning outcomes being assessed and is clearly stated.

- Measurable – the task can be measured against the standards/learning outcomes, allowing any gaps to be identified.

- Achievable – the task can be achieved at the right level.

- Realistic – the task is relevant and will give consistent results.

- Time bound – target dates or time limits are agreed.

Planning SMART assessment activities will ensure all the criteria will be met by your learners, providing they have acquired the necessary skills and knowledge.

Activity

Look at the syllabus for the subject/qualification you will assess. Can you produce sufficient materials or activities to ensure your learners will meet the assessment requirements, and that they are SMART?

Assessment planning should provide opportunities for both you and your learners to obtain and use information about progress towards the required outcomes. It should also be flexible in order to respond to any emerging ideas and skills, for example the use of new technology. The way you plan should include strategies to ensure that your learners understand what they are working towards, and the criteria that will be assessed. You should also plan how and when you will give your learners feedback. It could be verbally immediately after the assessment, the next time you see them, or by e-mail or another written means.

> *As part of effective teaching and learning, learners themselves also need to be actively engaged in the assessment process, identifying what it is they need to learn and develop.*

> www.qca.org.uk/qca_3293.aspx

Assessment planning should be short term and long term, to allow for formative and summative assessment to take place. Including your learners in the planning process will help identify what they have learnt, how and when they will be assessed, and allow for communication to take place to clarify any points or concerns. Encouraging an open dialogue will help learner motivation, and build up a climate of trust. Enabling your learners to self assess themselves against the relevant criteria will help them identify their own strengths and limitations, providing opportunities for further development if necessary.

Example

Rafael is due to assess one of his learners, Sabia, in her place of work. Sabia must meet the stated assessment criteria over a period of time for each unit of the qualification. She has carried out a self-assessment and feels that she is now ready to be formally assessed. A suitable date and time has therefore been agreed to tie in with the work Sabia will be doing which will confirm her competence.

When planning to assess, you should have a *rationale*; consider: *who, what, when, where, why* and *how* (WWWWWWH). This information should always be conveyed to your learners, to alleviate any confusion. If you are assessing on an individual basis, the assessment planning process should be formalised, and an *assessment plan* completed and agreed. The plan should reflect what will be assessed, by whom, where and when the assessment will take place, why it is taking place, and how it will take place.

Example

Who – Jenny the assessor, Irene the learner and Laurence the workplace supervisor.

What – level 1 in Sport, Recreation and Allied Occupations, unit 3, element 1, criteria 1–5.

When – Tuesday 14 May at 2 p.m.

Where – County Leisure Centre.

Why – to formatively assess competence.

How – observation and questioning, witness testimony.

The above would be formally agreed using an assessment plan pro-forma, which both assessor and learner should sign and date. When the assessment takes place, the plan will be updated to reflect what has been achieved. Using the WWWWWH approach, will ensure you are setting SMART targets with your learners.

You will need to take into account the possible contribution of any other people involved in the assessment process, for example, line managers or colleagues. You could assess more than one learner on the same day if they both work in the same office; this would be more cost effective than assessing on two different occasions.

The assessment plan is like a written contract between you and your learner, towards the achievement of their qualification. It can be reviewed, amended and updated at any time.

Some assessments will not require a formal assessment plan, but you must always be SMART when setting assessment activities, and discuss the process with your learners.

Example

Gabriel is due to assess her group's interviewing skills. She has informed them she will carry out an observation using a checklist during next week's session. The checklist covers the assessment criteria and clearly states what each learner must demonstrate, within a five minute interview. Gabriel has therefore been SMART with her assessment planning, and will give immediate feedback to her learners afterwards.

When planning assessments, you will need to take into account equality of opportunity, inclusivity and differentiation within the assessment process; see Chapter 3 for further details.

Being prepared will ensure you are organised and professional, and can act quickly if you need to. All learners are entitled to a fair assessment and should be given the best opportunity to demonstrate their ability. Whichever type and methods of assessment you choose, you need to treat each learner as an individual as their needs may be different.

Example

If you have a dyslexic learner it may be appropriate to ask questions rather than give a written test, or have someone to scribe their responses. For a partially sighted learner you could give papers in a larger font or use a magnified reading lamp. For a deaf learner, you could give a written test instead of an oral test. For a learner with Asperger's syndrome, you could use written questions rather than oral questions. For some learners who might struggle with spelling and grammar, the use of a computer could help. An adapted keyboard or a pen grip could help a learner with arthritis.

Some learners may have barriers to assessment, for example access to a particular room, transport or health problems. Some learners may require additional support with literacy and numeracy. You may also have to challenge your own values and beliefs if you don't agree with those of your learners to ensure you remain professional at all times. Some learners may have a support assistant who will be present during the assessment. They will be there to help your learner in case they have any difficulties. Make sure you address your learner, not their assistant, to ensure you are including them fully in the process. If you have a learner with a speech impediment, give them time to finish speaking before continuing.

Some examples of meeting your learners' needs are:

- adapting or providing specialist staff, resources and equipment;
- adapting the environment;
- allowing extra time;

- arranging to use another language (e.g. Welsh, British sign language);
- changing the date and/or time;
- identifying transferable skills;
- liaising with others who could offer advice or technical support;
- maintaining constant contact and support, for example via e-mail;
- providing specialist support;
- providing the assessment information in an alternative format;
- using a different location which is more accessible;
- using different assessment types and methods to suit learning styles;
- using larger print, Braille or other alternative support mechanisms;
- using ICT and new and emerging technologies.

Activity

Look at the assessment activities you are going to use with your learners: what support might you give to your learners, based upon their needs, and how would you go about arranging this?

You might be familiar with what you can and cannot do, but may need to find out whom you should liaise with to make appropriate arrangements. Always check with your organisation and Awarding/Examining body to ensure you are following their regulations. You cannot change a set examination date and time without approval, and may need consent in writing for other changes or amendments.

If you have a learner requiring support for any reason, there is a difference between *learning support* and *learner support*. Learning support relates to the subject, or help with language, literacy, numeracy or information communication technology (ICT) skills. Learner support relates to any help your learner might need with personal issues, and/or general advice and guidance.

Always ask your learners how you can help them, but try to avoid making them feel different or uncomfortable. If you are unsure of what you can do to help your learners, ask your supervisor or manager at your organisation. Don't just assume you are on your own to carry out any amendment to provision; there will be specialist staff to help.

Activity

Think about your learners and the environment in which you will be assessing them. Do you need to ask your learners if any adaptations or changes are required? Will the timing of the assessments impact on your learners in any way, for example during an evening session when they may not have had time to eat?

Never assume everything is fine just because your learners don't complain. Always include your learners in the assessment planning process in case there is something you don't know that you need to act upon.

When planning assessment activities, you need to know when your learners are ready. There's no point assessing them if they haven't learnt everything they need to know, as you will be setting them up to fail. If your learner has been absent for any reason, make sure you update them regarding what they have missed. Carrying out a formative assessment well before a summative assessment can help both you and your learner see how ready they are.

The timing of your assessments can also make a difference, if you plan to assess on a Friday before a holiday period, your learners may not be as attentive; equally so first thing on a Monday morning. This is difficult of course if you see your learners only on these particular days. If you are planning a schedule of assessments throughout the year, you will need to consider any public or cultural holidays. There is no point planning to assess every third Monday if the majority of these fall on public holidays. You might also need to assess your learner in their place of work. If they work shifts or during the weekend you would need to visit when they are working, as it isn't fair to ask them to change their work patterns just to suit you. If for any reason an assessment is cancelled, make sure a revised date is scheduled as soon as possible, and inform all concerned and update the assessment plan.

Assessment planning is a crucial part of the teaching and learning process. If this is not carried out correctly and comprehensively, problems may occur which could disadvantage your learners and prevent them from being successful.

Summary

In this chapter you have learnt about:

- types of assessment;
- assessment planning.

References and further information

Bloom, B.S. (1956) *Taxonomy of Educational Objectives, the Classification of Educational Goals – Handbook I: Cognitive Domain.* New York: McKay.

Gravells, A. and Simpson, S. (2008) *Planning and Enabling Learning.* Exeter: Learning Matters.

Ollin, R. and Tucker, J. (2008) *The NVQ Assessor, Verifier and Candidate Handbook* 4th edn. London: Kogan Page.

Websites

Assessment guidance booklets – www.sflip.org.uk/assessment/assessment guidance.aspx

Initial Assessment Tools – www.toolslibrary.co.uk

Literacy and Numeracy online tests – www.move-on.org.uk

Qualifications and Curriculum Authority – www.qca.org.uk

Quality Improvement Agency – http://excellence.qia.org.uk

Introduction

In this chapter you will learn about:

- methods of assessment;

- equality and diversity within assessment;

- making assessment decisions.

There are activities and examples to help you reflect on the above which will assist your understanding of the various methods of assessment, and how to make assessment decisions.

This chapter contributes towards the following: scope (S), knowledge (K) and practice (P) aspects of the professional standards (A–F domains) for teachers, tutors and trainers in the Lifelong Learning Sector.

AS1, AS2, AS3, AS5, AS6;
AK3.1, AK5.1, AK5.2, AK6.1, AK6.2;
AP1.1, AP2.1, AP3.1, AP5.1, AP5.2, AP6.1, AP6.2;
BS1, BS3, BS4, BS5;
BK1.1, BK1.3, BK2.2, BK3.2, BK3.5, BK4.1, BK5.2;
BP1.1, BP1.3, BP2.1, BP2.2, BP2.5, BP3.1, BP3.5, BP4.1, BP5.1, BP5.2;
CK3.2, CK3.3, CK3.5;
CP1.1, CP3.5, CP4.2;
DS1;
DP1.1;
ES1, ES2, ES3;
EK1.2, EK1.3, EK2.1, EK2.2, EK2.3, EK2.4, EK3.1, EK3.2, EK5.1, EK5.2, EK5.3;
EP1.1, EP1.2, EP1.3, EP2.1, EP2.2, EP2.3, EP3.1, AP3.2, EP5.5.

This chapter contributes towards the following A1 and A2 standards:

A1.1d, A1.1e, A1.1g, A1.1j;
A1.2a, A1.2d, A1.2f, A1.2g, A1.2h;
A1.3d, A1.3g.

A2.1a, A2.1b, A2.1c, A2.1d;
A2.2e, A2.2f, A2.2g, A2.2h;
A2.3a, A2.3b, A2.3c, A2.3e;
A2.4a, A2.4c, A2.4f.

Methods of assessment

There are several different ways of assessing to ensure learning has taken place; for example, observation, questioning, tests and exams. If these activities are not provided by the Awarding/Examining body you will need to devise your own. You would take into account your learners' needs, their level, and the subject requirements before planning a suitable method. Assessment can only take place once learning has occurred.

Activity

Think about the learners you have at present, or those whom you will be assessing in the future. How do you know that learning has taken place?

You might be able to answer this by saying, *I'll ask questions,* or *I'll see them working.* That's fine, if you know what questions to ask and how your learners should respond, or what you expect to see your learners do. To effectively plan how you will assess your learners, you need to use a method which is valid and reliable. If you set a test which doesn't accurately reflect the assessment criteria, it will be invalid. If you devise a set of questions, and use them with different groups of learners, they may discuss these amongst themselves, therefore rendering the questions unreliable.

Assessment can take place at any point in your learners' progress. Initial assessment will give you an appropriate starting point for your learners, giving you information about their skills and knowledge to date. Formative assessment helps you see how your learners are progressing, before moving on to other topics. It also helps you adapt your teaching to cover any additional work which might be necessary. Summative assessment will give a final decision as to your learners' achievements. If you are assessing your learners during a teaching session, remember to allow plenty of time for this when preparing your scheme of work and session plans.

If possible, try to incorporate the use of new and emerging technologies, and information communication technology (ICT), such as:

- a virtual learning environment (VLE);
- blogs, chat rooms and online discussion forums;
- computer facilities for the word processing of assignments;
- digital media for visual/audio recording;
- e-mail;
- the internet for research;
- mobile phone for taking pictures and video clips;
- web cameras or video conferencing if you can't be in the same place as your learners.

In March 2005 the Department for Education, Children's Services and Skills published the e-Strategy *Harnessing Technology: Transforming learning and children's services.* This strategy describes the use of digital and interactive technologies to achieve a more personalised approach within all areas of education and can be accessed at: www.dcsf. gov.uk/publications/e-strategy/.

Assessment should never be *just for the sake of assessing.* There should always be a reason for any assessment activity you carry out, the main one being to find out if learning has taken place.

Activity

Design an assessment activity to use with your learners, preferably incorporating ICT. This could be a formative activity to test progress to date. Use it with your learners and then evaluate how effective it was.

You might have found it easy to design the activity, but when you used it with your learners, it wasn't as effective as you would have liked. You need to take into account:

- any specific requirements within the syllabus;
- equality and diversity;
- the criteria you are assessing;
- the environment, facilities and resources;
- the need to be specific, measurable, achievable, realistic and time bound (SMART);
- the abilities, levels and needs of your learners;
- the reliability and validity of the type and method used;
- *who, what, when, where, why* and *how* (WWWWWH) you will assess.

Never be afraid to try something different, particularly with formative assessments that you can design yourself. You could use puzzles, quizzes or crosswords as a fun and active way of informally assessing learner progress. Try searching the internet for free software to help you create these.

Activity

Consider how you will assess your learners, taking into account the previous bullet points.

You might have thought about using different types and methods to give a varied approach to address all learning styles. You might use a *blended* approach to incorporate the use of technology with other methods. If you have different levels of learners within the same group, you could use the same activities, but with different assessment criteria, for example *list, describe, explain,* or *analyse.*

The results obtained from any assessment activity should be used to adapt and improve both your teaching and learning. Assessment should reinforce learning as well as measuring what has been learnt.

Assessment can be separated into the needs of the learner, the assessor, the organisation and the Awarding/Examining body.

Learner – to:

- clarify what is expected of them;
- enable discussions with assessors;
- evaluate their own progress;
- have something to show for their achievements, for example a certificate;
- know how well they are doing;
- know they are achieving the correct standard or level;
- know what they have to do next;
- learn from mistakes.

Assessor – to:

- adapt teaching and learning;
- ascertain progress so far;
- certificate learning;
- decide what's next;
- develop learners' self assessment skills;
- diagnose any learner needs or particular learning requirements;
- empower learners to take control of their learning;
- follow the requirements of the Awarding/Examining body;
- grade learners;
- improve motivation and self esteem;
- prepare learners for further assessments;
- prove they can assess effectively;
- recognise efforts and achievements;
- share judgements and practice with others;
- structure stages of progress.

Organisation – to:

- analyse enrolment, retention and achievement rates;
- achieve funding;
- ensure consistency between assessor practice;
- give references for learners if requested;
- identify gaps in learning;
- justify delivery of programmes;
- maintain records;
- promote a learner centred approach;
- satisfy Awarding/Examining body requirements;
- standardise decisions between assessors.

Awarding/Examining body – to:

- accredit achievements;
- ensure compliance with regulations and qualification requirements;
- set standards.

The table on page 42 lists the assessment methods and activities you could use, with a brief description, and the advantages and limitations of each. When using any activities, you need to ensure they are inclusive, and differentiate for individual learning styles and needs, learner difficulties and/or disabilities. Always follow health and safety guidelines, and carry out any relevant risk assessments where applicable. Make sure your learners are aware *why* they are being assessed, and don't over-complicate your activities.

Method	Description	Advantages	Limitations
Accreditation of prior learning (APL)	Assessing what has previously taken place to find a suitable starting point for further assessments	Ideal for learners who have achieved aspects of the programme prior to commencement No need for learners to duplicate work, or be reassessed	Checking the authenticity and currency of the evidence provided is crucial Can be time consuming for both your learner to prove, and the assessor to assess
Assignments	Several activities or tasks, practical or theoretical, to assess various aspects of a qualification over a period of time	Can challenge your learner's potential or consolidate learning A well-written project will help your learner provide evidence of knowledge and skills Some assignments are set by the Awarding/ Examining body and will have clear marking criteria for you to follow	If set by an Awarding/Examining body, ensure all aspects of the syllabus have been taught beforehand Must be individually assessed and written feedback given, which can develop learning further
Blended assessments	Using more than one method of assessment, usually including technology	Several methods of assessment can be combined, enabling all learning styles to be reached	Not all learners may have access to the technology
Buzz groups	Short topics to be discussed in small groups	Allows learner interaction and focuses ideas Checks understanding Doesn't require formal feedback	Learners may digress Specific points could be lost Checking individual learning has taken place may be difficult
Case studies/scenarios	Can be a hypothetical situation, a description of an actual event or an incomplete event, enabling learners to explore the situation	Can make topics more realistic, enhancing motivation and interest Can be carried out individually or in a group situation Builds on current knowledge and experience	If carried out as a group activity, roles should be defined, and individual contributions assessed, allow time for a de-brief to include a group discussion Must have clear outcomes Can be time consuming to mark

Method	Description		
Checklists	A list of criteria which must be met to confirm competence or achievement	Can form part of an ongoing record of achievement or profile Assessment can take place when your learner is ready Ensures all criteria are met and a record maintained	Learners may lose their copy and not remember what they have achieved
Discussions/debates	Learners talk about a relevant topic which contributes to the assessment criteria	All learners can participate Allows freedom of view points, questions and discussions	Easy to digress Assessor needs to keep the group focused and set a time limit Some learners may not get involved, others may take over – assessor needs to manage the contributions of individuals Can be time consuming Learners may need to research a topic in advance Can lead to arguments
e-assessments/ online assessments	*Electronic assessment* – assessment using information and communication technology (ICT) *Synchronous* – assessor and learner are simultaneously present, communicating in real time *Asynchronous* – assessor and learner are interacting at different times	Teaching, learning and assessment can take place in a virtual learning environment (VLE) Assessment can take place at a time to suit learners Participation is widened Results can be instantly generated Ensures reliability Less paperwork for the assessor Improves ICT skills Can be blended with other assessment methods Groups, blogs, forums and chat rooms can be set up to improve communication	Learners need access to a computer and need to be computer literate Self discipline is needed, along with clear targets Authenticity of learners' work may need validating Technical support may be required Reliable internet connection needed

Method	Description	Advantages	Limitations
Essays	A formal piece of written text, produced by your learner, for a specific topic	Useful for academic subjects Can check your learners' language and literacy skills at specific levels	Not suitable for lower level learners Marking can be time consuming Plagiarism can be an issue Doesn't usually have a right or wrong answer therefore difficult to grade Learners need good writing skills
Exams	A formal test which should be carried out in certain conditions	Can be open book, or open notes, enabling learners to have books and notes with them Some learners excel under pressure	Invigilation required Security arrangements to be in place prior to, and afterwards Learners may have been taught purely to pass expected questions by using past papers, therefore they may forget everything afterwards Some learners may be anxious
Group work	Enables learners to carry out a specific activity, for example problem solving Can be practical or theoretical	Allows interaction between learners Encourages participation and variety Rotating group members enables all learners to work with each other	Careful management by the assessor is required regarding time limits, progress, and ensuring all group members are clear about the requirements Could be personality problems with team members or large groups One person may dominate Difficult to assess individual contributions Time is needed for a thorough de-brief and feedback
Homework	Activities carried out between sessions, for example answering questions to check knowledge	Learners can complete at a time and place that suits them Maintains interest between sessions Encourages learners to stretch themselves further Consolidates learning so far	Clear time limits must be set Learners might not do it, or get someone else to do it for them Must be marked/assessed and individual feedback given

Icebreakers/team building exercises	A fun and light hearted way of introducing learners and topics	A good way of learners getting to know each other, and for the assessor to observe skills and attitudes Can revitalise a flagging session	Not all learners may want to take part Some learners may see these as insignificant – careful explanations are needed to link the experience to the topic
Interviews	A one to one discussion, usually before your learner commences a programme, or part way through to discuss progress	Enables the assessor to see how much a learner knows Enables the assessor to get to know each learner, and discuss any issues	Not all learners may react well when interviewed Needs careful planning, and consistency of questions between learners
Journal/diary	Learners keep a record of their progress, their reflections and thoughts, and reference these to the assessment criteria	Develops self assessment skills Relates theory to practice Helps assess language and literacy skills Useful for higher level programmes	Should be specific to the learning taking place and be analytical rather than descriptive Contents need to remain confidential Can be time consuming to read
Observations	Watching learners perform a skill	Enables skills to be seen in action Learners can make a mistake (if it is safe) enabling them to realise what they have done wrong Can assess several aspects of a qualification at the same time (holistic)	Timing must be arranged to suit your learner, communication needs to take place with others (if in your learner's workplace)
Peer assessments	Learners giving feedback to their peers after an activity	Enables learners to assess each other Promotes learner involvement Activities can often correct misunderstandings and consolidate learning without intervention by the assessor	There may be personality clashes resulting in subjective decisions Needs careful management and training in how to give feedback

Method	Description	Advantages	Limitations
Portfolios of evidence	A formal record of evidence (manual or electronic) produced by learners towards a qualification	Ideal for learners who don't like formal exams Can be compiled over a period of time Learner centred, promotes autonomy	Authenticity and currency to be checked Computer access required to assess electronic portfolios Tendency for learners to produce a large quantity of evidence All evidence must be cross referenced Can be time consuming to assess Confidentiality of documents within the portfolio must be maintained
Practical activities/tasks	Assesses learners' skills in action	Actively involves learners	Some learners may not respond well to practical activities Can be time consuming to create
Presentations	Learners deliver a topic, often using audio-visual aids	Can be individual or in a group Can assess skills, knowledge and attitudes	If a group presentation, individual contributions must be assessed Some learners may be nervous or anxious Practice sessions are useful, but time consuming
Products	Evidence produced by learners to prove competence, for example, paintings, models, video, audio, photos	Assessor can see the final outcome Learners feel a sense of achievement, for example, by displaying their work in an exhibition	Authenticity needs to be checked if the work in progress has not been seen
Professional discussions	A conversation between the assessor and learner based around the assessment criteria	Ideal way to assess aspects which are more difficult to observe Learners can describe how they carry out various activities	A record must be kept of the discussion, for example, audio tape and written notes Needs careful planning Assessor needs to be experienced at using open and probing questions, and listening carefully to the responses

Method	Description	Considerations
Projects	A longer-term activity enabling learners to provide evidence which meets the assessment criteria	Clear outcomes must be set, along with a time limit, must be relevant, realistic and achievable Progress should be checked regularly If a group is carrying out the project, ensure each individual's input is assessed Thorough feedback should be given
Puzzles, quizzes, word search, crosswords, etc.	A fun way of assessing learning in an informal way Fun activities to test knowledge, skills and/or attitudes Useful backup activity if learners finish an activity earlier than planned Useful way to assess progress of lower level learners Good for assessing retention of facts	Can seem trivial to mature learners Does not assess your learners' level of understanding or ability to apply their knowledge to situations Can be time consuming to create
Questions	A key technique for assessing understanding and stimulating thinking Questions can be closed, hypothetical, leading, open, probing, multiple choice etc. Can be written or oral, short or long answer Can challenge learners' potential A question bank can be devised which could be used again and again for all learners Can test critical arguments or thinking and reasoning skills	Closed questions only give a yes or no response which doesn't demonstrate knowledge Questions must be unambiguous If the same questions are used with other learners, they could share the answers Expected responses need to be produced beforehand May need to re-phrase some questions if learners are struggling with an answer (poor answers are often the result of poor questions)
Reports, research and dissertations	Learners produce a document to inform, recommend and/or make suggestions based on the assessment criteria Useful for higher level learners Encourages the use of research techniques	Learners need research and academic writing skills Time consuming to mark Plagiarism and authenticity can be an issue

Method	Description	Advantages	Limitations
Role plays	Learners act out a hypothetical situation	Enables you to observe learners' behaviour Encourages participation Can lead to debates Links theory to practice	Can be time consuming Clear roles must be defined Not all learners may want, or be able to participate Some learners may get too dramatic Individual contributions must be assessed
Self assessment	Learners decide how they have met the assessment criteria, or are progressing at a given time	Promotes learner involvement and personal autonomy Encourages learners to check their own work before handing in Learners need to be specific about what they have achieved and what they need to do to complete any gaps	Learners may feel they are doing better than they actually are Assessor needs to discuss progress and achievements with each learner to confirm their decisions
Simulation	Imitation or acting out of an event or situation	Useful when it is not possible to carry out a task for real, for example, to assess whether learners can successfully evacuate a building in a fire. You don't need to set fire to the building to observe this process	Only enables an assessment of a hypothetical situation; learners may act very differently in a real situation Not usually accepted as NVQ evidence
Tests	A formal assessment situation	Cost effective method as the same test can be used with large numbers of learners Some test responses can be scanned into a computer for marking and analysis	Needs to be carried out in supervised conditions Time limits required Can be stressful to learners and does not take into account any formative progress Feedback may not be immediate If set by an Awarding/Examining body, ensure all aspects of the syllabus have been taught before issuing the test Learners in other groups might find out the contents

Method	Description	Advantages	Disadvantages
Tutorials	A one to one, or group discussion between the assessor and learner, with an agreed purpose such as assessing progress so far	A good way of informally assessing learners' progress and/or giving feedback An opportunity for learners to discuss issues or for informal tuition to take place	Needs to be in a comfortable, safe and quiet environment as confidential issues may be discussed Time may overrun Records should be maintained and action points followed up
Video/Audio	Recorded evidence of actual achievements	Direct proof of what was achieved by learners Can be reviewed by the assessor, internal verifier/moderator after the event	Can prove expensive to purchase equipment and tapes/discs Can be time consuming to set up Technical support may be required Storage facilities are required
Walk and talk	A spoken and visual way of assessing learners' competence	Enables learners to *walk and talk* through their product evidence within their place of work Gives an audit trail of the evidence relating to the assessment criteria Saves time producing a full portfolio of evidence: the walk and talk can be recorded as evidence of the discussion Useful where sensitive and confidential information is dealt with	A time consuming way of assessing the criteria Difficult for verifiers to sample the evidence
Witness testimonies	A statement from a person who is familiar with your learner	The witness can confirm competence or achievements, providing they are familiar with the assessment criteria, for example a workplace supervisor	The assessor must confirm the suitability of the witness and check the authenticity of any statements
Worksheets and gapped handouts (known as *cloze sentence* or *missing words*)	Interactive handouts to check knowledge (can also be electronic) Blank spaces can be used for learners to fill in the missing words	Informal assessment activity which can be done individually, in pairs or groups Useful for lower level learners Can be created at different degrees of difficulty to address differentiation	Mature learners may consider them inappropriate Too many worksheets can be boring, learners might not be challenged enough

Equality and diversity within assessment

All learners should have equality of opportunity within assessment, providing they are taking a programme they are capable of achieving. There's no point setting learners up to fail, just because you needed a certain number of learners for your programme to go ahead. When designing assessment activities, you need to ensure you meet the needs of all your learners, and reflect the diverse nature of your group. Never let your own attitudes, values and beliefs interfere with the assessment process. You need to cover all the required assessment criteria, but you could design activities which will challenge more able learners and/or promote the motivation of learners who are not progressing so well. You need to differentiate your activities to ensure you are meeting the needs of all your learners, whilst adhering to any organisational and Awarding/Examining body requirements. Your organisation will have an Equal Opportunities or Equality and Diversity policy which you should become familiar with. You might have a learner who achieves tasks quickly; having more in-depth activities available and ready to use would be beneficial to them. If you have learners who are not achieving the required assessment tasks, design an activity that you know they will achieve, to raise their motivation and encourage them to progress. However, don't over simplify activities which will leave learners thinking they were too easy. You could always give your learners a choice of, for instance, a straightforward, a challenging or a very challenging activity. The choice may depend upon the confidence level of your learners, and you will have to devise such activities beforehand if they are not provided for you. If you have different levels of learners within the same group, this can work quite well as they will usually want to attempt something they know they can attain. However, it can also have the opposite effect in that learners feel they are more capable than they actually are.

Example

Elaine is assessing her group of learners for the Preparing to Teach Award. She has a mixed group of level 3 and level 4 learners. All of the learners opt to take the level 4 assessment tasks. However, once Elaine marks their responses, she realises most of them only meet the criteria for level 3. When she informs them of this, they do not take the feedback well.

In this example, all the learners felt they were capable of a higher level of achievement, and were therefore demoralised when told they were not to the required standard. If an initial assessment had been carried out beforehand, the learners would be aware of their abilities.

Assessment activities should always reflect the diverse nature of the group, for example, culture, language and ethnicity. They should not be biased according to the person producing them; otherwise aspects such as terminology or jargon might not be those of the learners, but those of the producer, placing the learner at a disadvantage. You also need to be careful not to discriminate against your learner in any way.

Example

Jo has a group of 20 learners taking a programme in photography. The learners are aged between 16–70, with a variety of religions and cultural backgrounds. They are mainly male and have various past experiences of the subject. Two of Jo's learners use a wheelchair, one is dyslexic and two have diabetes. For their next assignment, Jo has asked them to take a photograph of an object, one that represents something special to the learners. This assignment has been planned not to discriminate against anyone, and is therefore inclusive to all.

The Equality Act (2006) has replaced the Equal Opportunities Commission (EOC), the Commission for Racial Equality (CRE) and the Disability Rights Commission (DRC). To ensure you comply with the Act, you need to ensure you are proactive in all aspects of equality and diversity, and make sure your teaching, assessment and resources are inclusive in respect of *six strands*:

1　age;

2　disability;

3　gender;

4　race;

5　religion and belief;

6　sexual orientation.

Activity

Look at an assessment activity you will be using with your learners. Does it reflect the six strands? If not, can it be amended in any way to ensure it does, or at least reflect the community and society within which you assess?

Amendments could include using words like *person* instead of *man*, or using pictures in a handout to reflect different races. When designing activities, always try and take the six strands into account.

When planning assessments, you need to consider any particular requirements of your learners, to ensure they can all participate. Initial assessment would ensure your learners are able to take the subject; however, you may need to adapt resources, equipment or the environment to support them. If anything is adapted, make sure both you and your learners are familiar with them prior to carrying out the assessment activity. You cannot change the assessment criteria issued by the Awarding/Examining body, but you could change the way you implement the assessment process. If you need to make any changes, you must consult the relevant Awarding/Examining body to discuss these. Most will have an *Access to Assessment* document which will inform you what you can and cannot do.

Activity

Find out if your Awarding/Examining body has an Access to Assessment document, obtain a copy and have a look at the contents.

You can help your learners by organising your environment to enable ease of access around any obstacles (including other learners' belongings), along corridors, and around internal and external doors. When assessing, ensure you face your learners when speaking to assist anyone hard of hearing, produce clearly printed handouts in a font, size and colour to suit any particular learner requirements. Always ask your learners if there is anything you can do to help make the assessment experience a positive one.

Your organisation should have support mechanisms to meet any special assessment requirements or individual needs of learners.

Examples include learners with:

- dyslexia – allow additional time if necessary. Present written questions in a more simplified format, for example bullet points, or ask questions verbally and make an audio or visual recording of your learner's responses;

- a disability – learners could be assessed in a more comfortable environment where appropriate access and support systems are available. Learners could be given extra time to complete the assessment tasks, or to take medication privately. Dates could be rearranged to fit around doctor or hospital appointments;

- a hearing impairment – an induction loop could be used where all or part of an assessment is presented orally. Instructions and questions could be conveyed using sign language;

- a visual impairment – use large print or Braille, use specialist computer software if available, ask questions verbally and make an audio recording of your learner's responses;

- varying work patterns – try to schedule the assessment at a time and place to suit;

- English as a second or other language – if allowed, try to arrange assessments in your learner's first language, for example, in Welsh. Many Awarding/Examining bodies can translate assessment materials if requested.

All learners should have equality of opportunity and appropriate support to enable them to access assessment. Your organisation needs to ensure they follow the requirements of any relevant legislation such as the Disability Discrimination Act (DDA) 1995. The DDA was passed to protect disabled people from discrimination. According to the DDA, *a person has a disability if he or she has a physical or mental impairment, which has a substantial and long-term adverse effect on his/her ability to carry out normal day to day activities.*

Activity

Find out what support mechanisms are in place at your organisation, and who is responsible for arranging these, to meet any particular assessment requirements you may encounter.

It could be that you do not need to make any special arrangements just yet, but knowing what to do, and who to go to, will make things easier for you when the time does occur.

In September 2002 the DDA was extended to education, which broadened the rights of disabled people. Under Part 4 of the Act, colleges and Local Education Authorities (LEAs) have legal responsibilities:

- not to treat disabled learners less favourably for reasons related to their disability;

- to provide reasonable adjustments for disabled learners.

You need to anticipate the likely needs of disabled learners and not merely respond to individual needs as they arise. The Act uses a wide definition of disabled person to include: *people with physical or sensory impairments, dyslexia, medical conditions, mental health difficulties and learning difficulties.* Educational organisations have a duty to take reasonable steps to encourage learners to disclose a disability. This could be part of your learner application or interview process, and encouragement should be ongoing throughout the programme. If your learner does disclose a disability or additional need to anyone, including you as their assessor, then the whole organisation is *deemed to know*. It is therefore important that any issues are communicated to all other staff concerned, and acted upon.

From 2005, organisations have had to make *reasonable adjustments* to the physical features of their premises to overcome physical barriers to access. This could include the provision of ramps to classrooms, and access to disabled toilets. Desks are now available with adjustable legs which can be raised for wheelchair access, and specialist equipment is available to adapt resources. You may need further training to familiarise yourself with any particular assessment requirements to meet your learners' needs.

All assessments should be valid, authentic, current, sufficient and reliable (VACSR):

- valid – the work is relevant to the standards/criteria being assessed;

- authentic – the work has been produced solely by your learner;

- current – the work is still relevant at the time of assessment;

- sufficient – the work covers all the standards/criteria;

- reliable – the work is consistent across all learners, over time and at the required level.

This is particularly important if you are producing your own assessment activities. If you are writing a question paper, you need to ensure the questions fully meet the assessment requirements, and produce sample expected responses. This way, when you are marking, you have something to compare with. You would also have to be careful if you are using the same questions with different learners, in case they have the opportunity to discuss these.

You may assess learners of different ages, for example 14–19s with the new Diploma qualifications, 16 plus taking GCSEs or Advanced Levels, adults taking evening classes, or NVQs in their place of work. The way you deal with different age groups, and the types of assessment requirements you may have to deal with, will come with experience. You might also assess a group of learners at different levels of a qualification, and will need to differentiate your assessments accordingly.

Further details regarding equality and diversity can be found in the companion book by Gravells and Simpson (2009) *Equality and Diversity in the Lifelong Learning Sector.*

Making assessment decisions

To know that learning has occurred, some form of assessment must take place. A decision must then be made and a record kept. All decisions should be in accordance with the Awarding/Examining body requirements, and records must be maintained, usually for at least three years. It is quite a responsibility to confirm an achievement (or otherwise) as it can affect your learner's personal and professional development. Your learner may need to pass a qualification to achieve a promotion at work, or they may want to learn a new skill. To make a decision as to whether your learners have achieved, you need to ensure all the required assessment criteria have been met. You also need to be confident yourself that you understand what you are assessing.

Activity

Ask a colleague if you can observe an assessment session they are due to carry out. Look at the materials they use, how they communicate with their learners, how they reach their decisions, give feedback and complete their records.

Seeing how other assessors plan and assess will help you develop your own skills. Some qualifications may simply be achieved by a pass or a fail, for example a multiple choice test where learners must achieve seven out of ten for a pass. You would have a list of the correct responses, thus enabling you to mark objectively. You will also have regulations to follow in the event of a fail as to whether your learner can retake the test, and if so, when. Online testing often utilises multiple choice questions, and instant results can be given. It might not be a good idea to use tests with pass or fail for formative assessments, as negative results could demoralise your learners. However, if you feel they are useful, you could always use pass or refer: any learners with a refer result could have the opportunity to retake the same test, or an alternative one. It is harder to remain objective when learners are responding to open questions which do not have clear assessment criteria to follow.

Example

Haedish has a group of learners who need to pass at least eight out of ten questions to achieve a pass. The questions have been written by a team of staff within the organisation, but no expected responses have been provided. Haedish has been told to use her professional judgement to make a decision, but finds this difficult. She knows her learners are very capable, but they don't always express themselves clearly when writing. She has therefore decided that any learner who achieves a lower mark will not be referred, but will be given the opportunity to respond verbally to her.

In this example, Haedish has made a decision to differentiate for her learners. However she must first check with the other staff that this is acceptable, and if so, they must also be able to offer the same option. This will ensure that all assessors are being fair to all learners.

You may find, when assessing, that your learners haven't achieved everything they should have. When making a decision, you need to base this on all the information or evidence available to you at the time. If your learner has not met all the assessment criteria, you need to give constructive feedback, discuss any inconsistencies and give advice on what they should do next. If your learner disagrees with your decision, they are entitled to follow the appeals or complaints procedures. If you are having difficulty making a decision, discuss this with your line manager or a colleague to obtain a second opinion. You need to be fully confident when making decisions. You are not doing your learners any favours by saying they have achieved something when they haven't. You might also notice skills your learners have that they can use in other situations. It is useful to point out any such transferable skills to help them realise other contexts within which they can work. You may also see other aspects of the qualification requirements demonstrated, in addition to those planned.

If you are responsible for designing your own assessment activities and materials, you might decide to choose types and methods which are easy to mark. You might not have a lot of time for preparation and marking so the more time you spend preparing something suitable and relevant, the easier the marking will be.

Example

Charlotte sees her group of 18 learners once a week for three hours in a local community centre. She has written some scenarios, which have one correct answer out of three, to formatively assess their progress. As the time she spends with them is used to teach new skills and knowledge, she sets the scenarios as homework. The following week, she begins the session by asking the learners to swop their responses with a partner to mark, as she reads out the correct answers. This way, the marking is done for her, and a group discussion can then take place to clarify any anomalies.

This example works fine for the type of subject and maturity of learners. Experience will enable you to feel more confident with what suits your learners, their level and subject. You might feel uncomfortable trusting your learners to mark one another's, or even their own, work.

You might need to collaborate with other assessors, and make a joint decision regarding your learner's progress. Learners may act differently with other assessors, and you may see things that others hadn't. However, you must always remain objective; you are assessing your learner's competence towards set criteria, not their personality.

Activity

Consider what would influence you when making an assessment decision. Is the assessment criteria explicit, enabling you to be totally objective, or could it be misinterpreted, making it difficult for you to reach a decision?

If you feel it is difficult to make an objective decision with existing assessment activities, you will need to discuss your concerns with other staff, or with a contact from the Awarding/Examining body. If you are finding it difficult with activities or materials you have designed yourself, you will need to redesign these to make them more specific and unambiguous. If all your learners are achieving everything with ease, perhaps you are not being challenging enough.

If you are assessing a large amount of work from each learner, perhaps in the form of a portfolio or dissertation, it would be a good idea to have a system of signing this in and out. Your learner will have put a lot of effort into their work, and would like to know that you will take reasonable care with it. When you have made your decision and given feedback, you could ask your learner to sign that they have received it. If your learner was to lose their work, you should have your original assessment records to prove to the Awarding/Examining body that assessment has taken place.

Ensuring you choose the right method of assessment to carry out with your learners, and making an objective decision, will help your learners improve and achieve their aim.

Summary

In this chapter you have learnt about:

- methods of assessment;

- equality and diversity within assessment;

- making assessment decisions.

References and further information

DfES (2005) *Harnessing Technology: Transforming learning and children's services.* London.

LLUK (2007) *Addressing Literacy, Language, Numeracy and ICT Needs in Education and Training: Defining the minimum core of teachers' knowledge, understanding and personal skills.* London: Lifelong Learning UK.

Gravells, A. and Simpson, S. (2009) *Equality and Diversity in the Lifelong Learning Sector.* Exeter: Learning Matters.

Reece, I. and Walker, S. (2007) *Teaching, Training and Learning: A practical guide* 6th edn. Sunderland: Business Education Publishers Ltd.

Tummons, J. (2007) *Assessing Learning in the Lifelong Learning Sector* 2nd edn. Exeter: Learning Matters.

Websites

Assessment resources – www.questionmark.co.uk

Disability Discrimination Act – http://tinyurl.com/2vzd5j

Equality and Human Rights Commission – www.equalities.gov.uk

Lifelong Learning UK – www.lluk.org

Minimum Core Standards – http://tinyurl.com/6zmwcg

Puzzle software – www.about.com
                 www.crossword-compiler.com
                 www.educational-software-directory.net/game/puzzle
                 http://hotpot.uvic.ca
                 www.mathsnet.net

Teaching resources – http://excellence.qia.org.uk/golddust/

4 RECORDING PROGRESS

Introduction

In this chapter you will learn about:

- giving feedback;
- reviewing learner progress;
- assessment records.

There are activities and examples to help you reflect on the above which will assist your understanding of how to record progress.

Chapter 7 contains useful pro-formas you may wish to use.

This chapter contributes towards the following: scope (S), knowledge (K) and practice (P) aspects of the professional standards (A-F domains) for teachers, tutors and trainers in the Lifelong Learning Sector.

AS7;
AK5.1, AK5.2, AK7.1;
AP1.1, AP2.1, AP2.2, AP5.1, AP7.1;
BS3, BS4;
BK1.2, BK1.3, BK2.2, BK2.5, BK3.2, BK3.5, BK4.1;
BP1.3, BP2.5, BP3.2, BP3.4, BP3.5, BP4.1;
CS2, CS3;
CP1.2, CP3.2, CP3.3, CP3.5, CP4.2;
ES2, ES3, ES4, ES5;
EK2.4, EK3.1, EK4.1, EK4.2, EK5.3;
EP3.1, EP4.1, EP4.2, EP5.1, EP5.2, EP5.5;
FP1.1, FP1.2, FP2.1, FP4.2.

This chapter contributes towards the following A1 and A2 standards:

A1.1i, A1.1l, A1.1m;
A1.2c, A1.2h, A1.2i;
A1.3a, A1.3b, A1.3c, A1.3d, A1.3e, A1.3f;
A1.4a, A1.4c.

A2.1g;
A2.2c, A2.2d, A2.2f, A2.2h, A2.2i,
A2.3d, A2.3f;
A2.4a, A2.4b, A2.4c, A2.4d, A2.4e.

Giving feedback

All learners need to know how they are progressing and what they have achieved. Feedback will help encourage and motivate them. This can be given formally after an assessment, perhaps, in writing, or informally by talking to your learner. When giving feedback in writing, it should always be written on the correct document, not just written on your learner's work, in case they lose it. You can of course make developmental notes on your learner's work, for example to correct spelling errors, or to make annotations to show you have read it. You must keep records of feedback to satisfy organisational and Awarding/Examining body requirements.

Feedback can also be informal and given during a teaching session, to individuals during a review or tutorial, or by telephone or e-mail. When giving feedback, you should always try to be constructive, specific and developmental with what you say. You also need to make sure you are not being ambiguous or vague. You need to be factual regarding the achievements towards the assessment criteria, not just give your opinion. It is important to keep your learners motivated, and what you say can help or hinder their progress and confidence.

Example

All Fatima's learners had passed the required assessment criteria for their first assignment. When marking these, Fatima just wrote pass, along with good on each piece of work. Although there were a few spelling and grammatical errors within them all, she did not correct any.

Whilst the learners were probably happy they had achieved a pass, they would not be aware what they could improve upon, what was *good* about it, or that they had made some mistakes. They would therefore continue to make these mistakes, as they would not know differently. It could be that Fatima didn't even spot the mistakes herself. However, you would not want to demoralise your learners by writing too much on their first assignment; a combination of written and oral feedback might be better to retain motivation.

> Feedback using constructive comments leads to improved performance – up by 33%. Marking using grades can have a negative effect on learner performance, particularly for low achievers.
> Butler (1988) *British Journal of Educational Psychology* 56 (51–63)

As part of the new teaching regulations, teachers need to achieve the *minimum core requirements* in language, literacy, numeracy and ICT skills. Improving your own skills and knowledge will therefore help support your learners. You can view a copy of the standards via the internet shortcut http://tinyurl.com/6zmwcg.

If you are writing feedback to be read by learners at a later date, you need to appreciate that *how* you write it may not be how they *read* it. It is easy to interpret words or phrases differently to what is intended, therefore, if you can, read the feedback to them at the time of returning their work. If you don't see your learners regularly, you could mark their work at home and e-mail feedback to them. If so, don't get too personal with this, keep to the facts but be as positive as possible to retain their motivation. If you are giving individual verbal feedback, consider when and where you will do this, so as not to embarrass your learner in any way, and to allow enough time for any questions. Feedback should be a two way process, allowing a discussion to take place to clarify any points and plan further actions if necessary. Consider your tone of voice and take into account your learner's non-verbal signals. You might give verbal feedback to a group regarding an activity; if so, make sure your feedback is specific to the group, and/or each individual's contributions. Your learners will like to know how they are progressing, and what they need to do to improve or develop further. Simple statements such as *well done* or *good* don't tell your learner *what* was *well done* or *good* about their work or how they can improve it. Using your learner's name makes the feedback more personal, and making the feedback specific enables your learner to see what they need to do to improve.

Example

Jeremy sees his learners once a fortnight; between times, he marks their assignments and e-mails informal feedback. A typical e-mail reads: *Paula, you have passed your assignment. I particularly liked the way you compared and contrasted the two styles of writing. Do be careful when proofreading, you tend to use were instead of where. I will return your assignment when I next see you, along with more detailed written feedback.*

This feedback is specific and developmental and will help Jeremy's learners to stay motivated until he next sees them. Giving feedback this way is also a good method of keeping in touch if you don't see your learners frequently, and gives your learners the opportunity to communicate with you if necessary. E-mails and written feedback enable you to maintain records, if required, for audit purposes. Feedback can lose its impact if you leave it too long, and learners may think you are not interested in their progress.

Activity

Think of an instance where you have given feedback recently: could you have improved this in any way? What did you find difficult about giving feedback?

There may have been issues such as not having enough time, or perhaps you are not very good with eye contact, or being specific and developmental. Giving constructive feedback comes with practice.

> If rich feedback is to be given to all learners, then tutors need the time to read and reflect on their assignments, time to write encouraging and stretching comments, and time to discuss these face to face.
>
> Coffield (2008:36)

The role of questioning in feedback allows your learner to consider their achievements before you tell them. A good way to start this is to ask your learner how they feel they have done. This gives them the opportunity to realise their own mistakes, or reflect on what they could do differently. You could then build on this through feedback, and discuss what needs to be achieved next.

Some hints when questioning:

● allow enough time;

● ask open questions, e.g., who, what, when, where, why and how;

● avoid trick questions;

● be aware of your posture, gestures and body language;

● be conscious of your dialect, pitch and tone;

● don't ask more than one question in the same sentence;

● involve everyone if you are talking to a group;

● try not to say *erm, yeah, okay, you know,* or *does that make sense?* (the latter may only gain a *yes* response as learners feel that is what you want to hear);

● use active listening skills;

● use eye contact;

● use learners' names;

● watch your learners' reactions.

Peer assessment and feedback can also be useful to develop and motivate learners. However, this should be managed carefully, as you may have some learners who do not get along, and might use the opportunity to demoralise one another. You would need to give advice to your learners as to how to give feedback effectively; for example, start with something positive, then state what could be improved, and finish on a positive note. If learner feedback is given skilfully, other learners may consider more what their peers have said than what you have. If you consider peer assessment has a valuable contribution to make to the assessment process, ensure you plan for it, to enable your learners to become accustomed and more proficient at giving it.

The advantages of giving constructive feedback are:

● it creates opportunities for clarification and discussion;

● it emphasises progress rather than failure;

● it gives your learner confidence;

● it identifies further learning opportunities or action required;

● it motivates your learner;

● your learner knows what they have achieved;

● your learner knows what they need to improve upon or change.

Feedback should always be adapted to the level of your learners. You won't help your learners if you are using higher level words or jargon, when their level of understanding is lower. You should also be aware of where you give the feedback, in case you are disrupted or in a noisy environment. You should always give feedback in a way which will make it clear how your learner has met the required outcomes, and what they need to do next.

Example

Hanna is working towards the level 1 Certificate in Contact Centre Skills. She has just been observed by her assessor Geoff, who has also marked her responses to the written questions. Geoff gave her verbal feedback stating: *Hanna, you've done really well and passed all the criteria for the observation and written questions. You dealt with the irate customer in a pleasant and calm way. However, I would recommend you use the customer's name a bit more when speaking with them to appear friendly. You've met all the requirements; we can now sign that unit off and plan for the next one.*

In this example, the assessor was specific, constructive and positive with his feedback; Hanna knew that she had achieved the unit, and what she could do to improve for the future. The use of the word *however* is much better than the word *but*, which sounds negative. The feedback was also worded at the right level for the learner.

Often, the focus of feedback is likely to be on mistakes rather than strengths. If something positive is stated first, any negative comments are more likely to be listened to and acted upon. Starting with a negative point may discourage your learner from listening to anything else that is said.

If assessment decisions count towards the achievement of a qualification, it is crucial you keep your feedback records, along with any action identified, for each learner. You might save these electronically, or file hard copies by learner surname. Records must always be kept safe and secure; your car boot is not a good idea, nor is a corner of the staffroom. Awarding/Examining bodies expect records to be securely managed. You should also maintain a tracking sheet to show the overall progress of all your learners towards the different aspects or units of the qualification. Example assessment records are available in Chapter 7.

Reviewing learner progress

It is important to review learner progress regularly. This gives you the opportunity to discuss on a one to one basis how they are progressing, what they have achieved, and what they may need to improve or work on in the future. Reviews are a good opportunity to carry out formative assessments in an informal way. They also give your learner the opportunity to discuss any concerns or ask questions they might have been self conscious about asking in a group situation. The review should be formally documented and signed, and should be carried out at a suitable time during the learning and assessment process. Informal reviews and discussions can take place at any opportune time. Reviewing progress enables you to differentiate effectively, ensuring that the needs of your learners are met, and that they are being challenged to develop to their full potential. It also helps you see when learners are experiencing any difficulties, enabling you to arrange for any necessary support or further training.

Reviewing progress enables you to:

- check skills and knowledge gained from a previous session, before commencing the current session;

- discuss any confidential or sensitive issues;

- discuss achievement of *functional skills* if applicable;

- give constructive and developmental feedback;

- keep a record of what was discussed;

- involve your learners, formally or informally;

- motivate your learners;

- plan for differentiation;

- plan future learning and assessments;

- plan more challenging or creative assessment opportunities;

- provide opportunities for further learning or support;

- review your own contribution to the learning and assessment process;

- revise your scheme of work and session plans;

- revise your strategies for assessment;

- update your learner's assessment plan.

Activity

Find out what is involved with the learner review process at your organisation. Is there a particular form you need to complete? Do you have to review all your learners regularly, for example monthly or termly? Can you carry out informal reviews at times to suit both you and your learners?

If there is no set procedure, or you are not required to review your learners, it would still be a useful activity to do if you have the time. When reviewing progress, you should revise or update your learner's assessment plan. The review process should be ongoing until your learner has completed their qualification. Regular reviews can help to keep your learners motivated, make them feel less isolated, and appreciate how they are progressing so far.

The review process should involve:

- arranging a suitable date, time, and location, and confirming these to your learner;

- communicating with anyone else involved in the assessment process prior to the meeting;

- obtaining all relevant records relating to your learner, the subject, and the assessments carried out;

- discussing any issues or concerns, progress and achievements so far;

- referring to the previous assessment plan;

- updating the assessment plan with achievements and dates;

- identifying any training needs;

- planning future assessment activities and target dates, ensuring these are SMART, along with the next review date;

- signing and dating the assessment plan, giving a copy to your learner.

Example

Richard has a group of 12 learners who are attending a weekly evening class from 7–9 p.m. for 30 weeks. He has decided to dedicate one session per ten weeks for individual tutorials and reviews. Whilst he is carrying these out, the rest of the group will work on current projects or use the organisation's library facilities. This enables Richard to discuss individual progress, concerns and actions with each learner. It also helps him plan and evaluate his teaching and assessment methods.

It could be that your learners reveal some personal problems to you. If you don't feel you can help, try to refer them to someone who can, or encourage them to seek advice elsewhere.

Activity

Find out what specialist support is available in your organisation for helping learners, for example counselling. Or what agencies you could refer your learners to. They may have an issue you cannot deal with, such as financial, medical, etc.

Always listen to what your learners have to say, without interrupting them; they may not have the opportunity elsewhere to talk to someone about sensitive issues. Always retain confidentiality of information your learners disclose to you, otherwise you could lose their trust and respect. However, you need to know where your boundaries as an assessor stop, and not get involved personally.

Example

Michael was reviewing the progress of his learner John, who was taking Advanced Level in History. John disclosed the fact that he had some problems at home which were impeding upon the agreed target dates. Michael asked if he would like to discuss these further, but John declined, simply asking for an extension date. Michael agreed to this, and they completed and signed the organisation's document for an extension.

You could always review the progress of your learners as a group. At an appropriate time during the programme hold a discussion regarding how they feel they are progressing. This is particularly useful when you need to assess group activities. It could be that some activities do not suit the learning styles of a few learners, therefore not enabling them to fully contribute. Using several different activities could alleviate this, and make the process more interesting. Feedback from group reviews can inform the assessment planning process, and also be a valuable tool to evaluate the programme as a whole.

When assessing and reviewing progress, always try and ensure that the environment meets your learners' basic needs, such as feeling safe and comfortable. This will enable them to feel secure enough to progress further. Maslow (1954) introduced a *Hierarchy of Needs*. These needs represent different levels of motivation and have been adapted by other theorists as time has progressed. The highest level was labelled *self-actualising*, meaning people were *fully functional*, possess a *healthy personality*, and *take responsibility* for themselves and their actions. Maslow also believed that people should be able to move through these needs to the highest level, providing they are given an education that promotes growth.

The following diagram shows the needs expressed as they might relate to learning.

Ensuring the assessment environment meets your learners' first level needs will enable them to feel comfortable and secure enough to learn and progress to the higher levels. You will need to appreciate that some learners may not have these lower needs met in their home lives, making it difficult for them to move on to the higher levels in their learning.

Using the correct type of assessment to suit your learners, carrying out careful and appropriate assessment planning and reviewing progress will ensure you are meeting the needs of your learners. You will also make sure your learners are on the right track to achieving a successful result.

Assessment records

It is important to keep records, otherwise how would you know what your learners have achieved? You also need to satisfy any organisational, quality assurance, Awarding/Examining and regulatory bodies' audit requirements. This will usually be for a set period, for example three years, and should be the original records, not photocopies or carbon copies. It is fine to give copies to your learners, as it is harder to forge a copy than an original. Sadly, there are learners who do this; therefore keeping the originals will ensure your records are authentic.

The types of records you might maintain include:

- assessment plan and review;
- assessment tracking sheet;
- enrolment form;
- feedback and action plan;
- individual learning plan;
- induction record;
- initial assessment;
- register;
- skills and knowledge report;
- standardisation record;
- tutorials.

You might use other documents which have different titles such as:

- application form;
- checklists;
- observation report;
- professional discussion record;
- record of oral questions;
- reports to parents/guardians/employers regarding progress;
- retention and achievement records;
- unit declarations;
- witness testimony.

There may be a standardised approach to completing the records, for example, the amount of detail which must be written, or whether the records should be completed electronically. Some organisations now use hand held computers to directly input information, and support their learners to produce their work electronically, for example an e-portfolio of evidence towards an NVQ.

Some records might be maintained centrally within your organisation using a management information system; these should include:

- learner details: name, address, date of birth, contact information, registration, enrolment, and/or unique learner number;

- assessor details: name, contact information, curriculum vitae, continuing professional development plans and records;

- schemes of work and session plans for taught programmes;

- internal and external verification/moderation reports;

- records of actions taken from the above reports;

- organisational self assessment reports;

- Awarding/Examining body syllabus or qualification handbook;

- regulatory and funding guidance;

- evaluation forms and survey results;

- appeals and complaints;

- statistics such as retention and achievement;

- equal opportunities data such as an analysis by ethnic origin, disability, gender and age.

Records can be paper based, electronic, or a mixture of the two. The Data Protection Act (1998) is mandatory for all organisations that hold or process personal data. The Data Protection Act contains *Eight Principles*, to ensure that data is:

1. processed fairly and lawfully;

2. obtained and used only for specified and lawful purposes;

3. adequate, relevant and not excessive;

4. accurate and, where necessary, kept up to date;

5. kept for no longer than necessary;

6. processed in accordance with the individual's rights;

7. kept secure;

8. transferred only to countries that offer adequate protection.

Confidentiality should be maintained regarding information. The Freedom of Information Act (2000) gives your learners the opportunity to request to see the information your organisation holds about them. All external stakeholders such as Awarding/Examining and funding bodies should be aware of your systems of record keeping as they may need to approve certain records or storage methods. All records should be accurate and legible; if you need to make any amendments, make crossings out rather than use correction fluid. Try and keep on top of your paperwork, even if this is carried out electronically. If you leave it a while, you may forget to note important points. You will need to be organised and have a system; learner records could be stored alphabetically in a filing cabinet, or in separate electronic folders on a computer. If storing electronically, make sure you keep a backup copy in case anything gets accidentally deleted. Other records could be stored by the programme or qualification title, Awarding/Examining body name, etc.

Example

Andrea has a group of 12 learners working towards a Health and Social Care qualification. She maintains an A4 lever arch file, which has a tracking sheet at the front to record each learner's completed units. She then has plastic wallets for each learner, filed alphabetically, which contain their assessment plans and reviews, skills and knowledge reports, along with feedback and action plans. She has a separate folder for the Awarding/Examining body standards and blank pro-formas. Each time she completes a pro-forma, she makes a copy to give to her learners.

When completing any records, if signatures are required, these should be obtained as soon as possible after the event if they cannot be signed on the day. Any signatures added later should have the date they were added, rather than the date the form was originally completed. If you are assessing an NVQ, the QCA Code of Practice (2006:13) states that a *written declaration* must be provided. This should use the wording ... *evidence is authentic and that assessment took place under the conditions or context set out in the assessment specification.* The Code of Practice then goes on to state ... *Failure to do this constitutes grounds for the suspension or withdrawal of approved status for the NVQ in question.* You can see that authenticity is an issue which must therefore be taken very seriously. If you are assessing your learners directly, for example by an observation, you will know who they are. If you are assessing work that has been handed to you on a different date, or sent electronically, you will need to ensure it is the work of your learner. Unfortunately, some learners copy or plagiarise the work of others. Sometimes this is deliberate, other times it is due to a lack of knowledge of exactly what was required, or a misunderstanding. If you feel the work that has been handed to you may not be the actual work of your learner, ask them some questions about it. This will confirm their knowledge, or otherwise. If you feel it isn't their work, you will need to confront them and let them know you will take the matter further. You will then need to inform your line manager or internal verifier/moderator of the situation, explaining to your learner that they have the right to appeal. At this point your learner may confess, they may have what they consider a legitimate excuse. However, you must be certain the work is theirs, otherwise it could be classed as fraud.

Example

Louise and Leanne are sisters, both taking a Certificate in Information Technology, which is assessed by assignments, completed in their own time. When their assessor marked their work, he discovered the answers from both, which had been word processed, were almost the same. He confronted them individually. Louise insisted the work was her own and had no idea why it looked similar to Leanne's. Leanne became quite upset and admitted to accessing Louise's files without her knowledge. She had been concerned at completing the work within the deadline. In this instance, the assessor credited Louise with the original work, and asked Leanne to re-do the assignment on her own.

It is easier to compare the work of your own learners; however, other assessors in your organisation may also assess the same programme with different learners. In this case, the internal verifier/moderator may pick up on issues when they are sampling. It is difficult to check and compare the work of all learners, therefore, the importance of authenticity must be stressed to your learners at the commencement of their programme, and continually throughout. Asking learners to sign and date their work is always useful, particularly where this has been prepared on a computer. Some other ways of checking the authenticity of learners' work include:

- syntax, spelling, grammar and punctuation – if you know your learner speaks in a certain way at a certain level, yet their written work does not reflect this;

- work that includes quotes which have not been referenced – without a reference source, this is direct plagiarism and could be a breach of copyright;

- word processed work that contains different fonts and sizes of text – this shows it could have been copied from the internet, or someone else's file;

- hand written work that looks different to your learner's normal handwriting, or is not the same style or language as normally used, or word processed work when they would normally write by hand;

- work that refers to information you haven't taught, or is not relevant to the assessment criteria.

Activity

Find out what your organisation's policy is regarding cheating, copying and plagiarism. Ensure all your learners are aware of it, and encourage them to sign and date all work submitted. This ensures they are taking ownership of their work.

The Copyright, Designs and Patents Act (1988) is the current UK copyright law. Copying the work of others without their permission would infringe the Act. Copyright is where an individual or organisation creates something as an original, and has the right to control the ways in which their work may be used by others.

Normally the person who created the work will own the exclusive rights. However, if the work is produced as part of your employment, for example, if you had produced several handouts or a workbook for your learners, then normally the work will belong to your organisation. Learners may be in breach of this Act if they plagiarise or copy the work of others without making reference to the original author.

If you are assessing the work of learners you might not have met, for example, by e-*assessment*, it can be very difficult to ensure the authenticity of their work. E-assessment systems often allow contact to take place between the learner and assessor through a website *platform*. You could communicate in this way, or via e-mail, and then compare the style of writing in the submitted work, to that within the communications.

If you are assessing a programme which is non-accredited, i.e. it is not externally accredited by an Awarding/Examining body, you will need to follow the requirements for recognising and recording progress and achievement in non-accredited learning (RARPA). There are five processes to RARPA:

1. aims – these should be appropriate to the individual or group of learners;

2. initial assessment – this should be used to establish each learner's starting point;

3. identification of appropriately challenging learning objectives – these should be agreed, renegotiated and revised as necessary after formative assessment, and should be appropriate to each learner;

4. recognition and recording of progress and achievement during the programme – this should include assessor feedback, learner reflection and reviews of progress;

5. end of programme – this includes summative assessment, learner self assessment and a review of overall progress and achievement. This should be in relation to the learning objectives and any other outcomes achieved during the programme.

If you use the RARPA system, you will need to check what records must be maintained; there may be a standard system for you to follow or you may need to design your own assessment records.

Record keeping and ensuring the authenticity of your learners' work is of paramount importance. To satisfy all the stakeholders involved in your programme or qualification, you must be able to show a valid audit trail for all your decisions.

Summary

In this chapter you have learnt about:

- giving feedback;

- reviewing learner progress;

- assessment records.

References and further information

Butler, R. (1988) Enhancing and undermining intrinsic motivation: effects of task-involving and ego-involving evaluation on interest and performance. *British Journal of Educational Psychology* 56 (51–63).

Coffield, F. (2008) *Just Suppose Teaching and Learning Became the First Priority.* London: LSN.

QCA (2006) *NVQ Code of Practice.* London: QCA.

Websites

Association for Achievement and Improvement through Assessment (AAIA) – www.aaia.org.uk/

Data Protection Act – www.ico.gov.uk/what_we_cover/data_protection.aspx

Functional Skills – http://www.qca.org.uk/qca_6062.aspx

Maslow – www.maslow.com

Plagiarism – www.plagiarism.org

RARPA – www.rarpatoolkit.com/en/rarpa.asp

UK Intellectual Property Office – www.ipo.gov.uk

Introduction

In this chapter you will learn about:

- internal quality assurance;

- appeals, complaints and disputes;

- standardisation of practice;

- external quality assurance.

There are activities and examples to help you reflect on the above which will assist your understanding of quality assurance within the assessment process.

Chapter 7 contains useful pro-formas you may wish to use.

This chapter contributes towards the following: scope (S), knowledge (K) and practice (P) aspects of the professional standards (A–F domains) for teachers, tutors and trainers in the Lifelong Learning Sector.

AS6, AS7;
AK5.1, AK6.1, AK6.2, AK7.1, AK7.2;
AP4.2, AP5.1, AP5.2, AP6.1, AP7.1, AP7.2;
BS4;
BK2.6;
BP4.1;
CS3;
CK1.1, CK4.1;
CP1.1, CP4.1;
ES2, ES3, ES5;
EK2.4, EK5.1, EK5.2, EK5.3;
EP2.4, EP5.1, EP5.2, EP5.5.

This chapter contributes towards the following A1 and A2 standards:

A1.1j;
A1.2d, A1.2f, A1.2j;
A1.3g;
A1.4b, A1.4d.

A2.1d, A2.1e;
A2.3e;
A2.4f.

Internal quality assurance

All programmes should have a quality assurance system to ensure they are being delivered and assessed fairly, consistently and accurately. There are various aspects of quality assurance which will take place internally within your organisation. These include:

- analysing enrolment, retention and achievement figures;
- compiling self assessment reports;
- ensuring policies and procedures are up to date;
- ensuring qualifications are fit for purpose and validated;
- facilitating appropriate staff development and training;
- implementing strategies for verification and moderation activities;
- interpreting qualification requirements correctly;
- interviewing learners;
- issuing questionnaires to learners and responding to feedback;
- maintaining records and audit trails;
- maintaining standards;
- monitoring appeals, complaints and disputes;
- observing assessment planning, decisions and feedback;
- preparing for external body visits and implementing action points;
- reviewing assessment requirements and strategies;
- setting targets or performance indicators.

You might not be involved with all of the above, but they will impact upon your role as an assessor. Your organisation should have a written quality assurance strategy which you should familiarise yourself with.

As an assessor, you should be supported by an internal verifier/moderator who will have overall responsibility for the quality of the programme. They will sample your assessed work and give you feedback. They will also ensure you are following Awarding/Examining body requirements, and are maintaining your professional development.

If your programme is verified, and a problem is found when sampling one of your assessment decisions, the internal verifier will give you advice as to how you can put things right with your learner. If your programme is moderated and a problem is found, all learners in your group will need to be reassessed.

Ewan had assessed his group of 12 learners for a Literacy qualification. When the internal moderator, Sheila, sampled two of his marked assignments, she noticed one of the questions had not been fully answered, yet Ewan had awarded a pass. When Sheila discussed this with Ewan, he realised he had not covered this topic fully with his learners. He therefore delivered the topic correctly the next time he had his group. The learners then had to resubmit their assignment for reassessment.

In this situation, the internal moderator was able to help the assessor, and ultimately his learners. If internal moderation had not taken place, the learners would have achieved a qualification, without successfully achieving all the assessment criteria. If the certificates had been claimed from the Awarding/Examining body, then this could be classed as fraud.

If you assess an NVQ in England, Wales or Northern Ireland, you must follow the *NVQ Code of Practice* produced by the Qualifications and Curriculum Authority. A copy can be located via their website (www.qca.org.uk).

If you assess a higher educational qualification, you will need to follow the *Code of practice for the assurance of academic quality and standards in higher education* produced by the Quality Assurance Agency (QAA). A copy can be located via their website (www.qaa.ac.uk).

> *In higher education, 'assessment' describes any processes that appraise an individual's knowledge, understanding, abilities or skills.*
>
> Code of practice for the assurance of academic quality and standards in higher education (2006 section 6 page 4)

Whether you assess a vocational or an academic subject, your assessment practice will be quality assured in line with a Code of Practice, and/or guidelines and regulations published by the relevant Awarding/Examining body. They will want to ensure you are maintaining the integrity of their name.

Locate a copy of the Code of Practice relevant to you, and the Awarding/Examining body requirements for quality assuring the programme you assess. Look at it to make sure you are being compliant. If you are unsure of any aspect, discuss this with your internal verifier/moderator.

There are other external bodies that will advise and monitor quality assurance; these will depend upon which area of the United Kingdom you are working in and whether your organisation receives external funding. They include:

- Learning and Skills Council (LSC);

- Local Education Authority (LEA);

- Office for Standards in Education, Children's Services and Skills (Ofsted);

- Office of the Qualifications and Examinations Regulator (Ofqual).

Sector Skills Councils (SSC) and Standards Setting Bodies (SSB) work with employers and partners to develop the standards for the qualifications you might be assessing. You can locate a copy of the standards and the details of the relevant Body via the Skills for Business website (www.ukstandards.org). Any revisions to the standards will be notified via their website and you can also obtain details regarding the assessment and quality assurance strategies. Internal quality assurance is crucial to the integrity of the qualification, and the reputation of your organisation.

Appeals, complaints and disputes

At some point during the assessment process, a learner may wish to appeal against one of your decisions, have a complaint, or dispute a grade you have given them. At the induction stage, you should have given your learners information that would enable them to follow your organisation's procedures. Information could also be displayed on notice boards, in the learner handbook, or be available via your organisation's intranet. Learners will need to know who they can go to, and that their issue will be followed up.

Activity

Locate and read your organisation's policies and procedures for appeals, complaints and disputes.

Some organisations will provide a pro-forma for learners to use, which ensures all the required details are obtained, or encourage an informal discussion first. Statistics should be maintained regarding all appeals and complaints; these will help your organisation when reviewing their policies and procedures, and should be provided to Awarding/Examining, regulatory, and funding bodies if requested.

Having a climate of respect and honesty can lead to issues being dealt with informally, rather than procedures having to be followed which can be upsetting for both parties concerned.

Complaints may be made against something you have or have not done. If your learner has a complaint, they might not feel confident to discuss it directly with you, but go to a third party.

Example

Jonas had received a pass from his assessor, Chika, for his recent assignment. He felt he had met the criteria for a distinction, but didn't discuss this with his assessor. He complained to another assessor, who informed Chika. At the next session, Chika asked Jonas if he agreed with the grade he received; he said he did.

In this situation, Jonas felt he deserved a higher grade, and complained to a third party, but when given the opportunity to discuss it, he said he agreed with it. This could be because there was a personality clash between the assessor and learner, or he really did agree with the grade, and just wanted to complain for the sake of it. If this happens to you, ask a colleague, or your internal verifier/moderator, to reassess the work. This will confirm whether or not you are correct, and if not, your learner should achieve the revised grade.

A complaint is often about a situation or a person, whereas an appeal or a dispute is about achievement. Learners who complain should be able to do so without fear of recrimination. Confidentiality should be maintained where possible to ensure an impartial decision. If any of your learners do have an appeal, complaint or dispute, this should not affect the way you or other learners or staff treat them. The outcome should not jeopardise your learner's current or future achievements. You should always remain professional in your role, to promote a positive assessment experience for all your learners.

Standardisation of practice

Standardisation ensures consistency and fairness of all assessment decisions. You may have to standardise your decisions with other assessors, particularly where more than one assessor is involved with the same subject. It is also a chance to ensure all assessors are interpreting the qualification requirements and assessment criteria correctly, and completing records appropriately. Attending a standardisation event will give you the opportunity to share good practice and compare your assessment decisions with your colleagues, by looking at their assessed work and vice versa. Even if you don't learn anything new, it will confirm you are doing things right. Standardisation events *are not* team meetings; the latter are to discuss issues relating to the management of the programme, for example, Awarding/Examining body updates, targets and achievements.

Example

Lukas was a new assessor, and was not very familiar with the revised standards of the qualification he was due to assess. The full team of assessors met once a fortnight to discuss the content of each unit, to ensure they were all interpreting it correctly. At this meeting, they would also swop units they had assessed, enabling the team to see how assessments had been planned, carried out and recorded. This prompted a discussion which ensured all the assessors could standardise their practice. Records were kept which could be referred to in case of a query, which greatly helped Lukas understand the standards.

If you are assessing an NVQ and don't carry out standardisastion activities, or insufficiently record the outcomes, your organisation will be given a *level two sanction* by your external verifier. The NVQ Code of Practice paragraph 48, states organisations must ensure:

> the accuracy and consistency of assessment decisions between assessors operating at the centre;

> that assessors are consistent in their interpretation and application of the national occupational standards in the award.

A level two sanction means your organisation cannot claim any certificates until the external verifier has sampled all the learners' assessed work.

The benefits of standardisation are:

- a contribution to continuing professional development;
- accountability to Awarding/Examining and external bodies;
- all assessment decisions are fair for all learners;
- an opportunity to discuss new standards;
- clearly defined roles and responsibilities;
- compliance with the NVQ Code of Practice;
- confirming your own practice and sharing good practice;
- spotting trends or inconsistencies;
- succession planning if assessors are due to leave;
- consistency and fairness of decisions;
- empowerment of assessors to take responsibility;
- to give an audit trail of aspects standardised;
- to give assessors time to formally meet to discuss assessments;
- to meet quality assurance requirements;
- to set action plans for the development of systems and staff.

Activity

Look at the qualification standardisation pro-forma in Chapter 7. Does your organisation use something similar? If not, use this form next time to ensure you are compliant.

You might use the term *double marking* rather than standardisation. This enables different assessors to mark one another's assessed work, to ensure the correct grade has been given. This might take place *blindly,* i.e. you don't get to see the grade already given. Having a *marking scheme* or *expected answers* will help you reach a fair decision. If standardisation was not carried out, assessment activities would not be fair to all learners. You might carry out three observations with your learners, and give them a written test, whereas another assessor might only carry out one observation and ask some questions orally. There are times when an individual learner's needs should be taken into account, which will lead to a difference in assessment activities. However, all learners should be entitled to the same assessment experience, no matter which assessor they are allocated to.

> Standardised summative assessments, marked in the same way for everyone, are necessary for any modern society, which aspires to fairness and justice for its citizens.
>
> Wolf (2008:19)

It's important to keep up to date with any changes to qualification standards. Awarding/Examining bodies issue regular updates, either by hard copy or electronically. Once you receive these, you need to discuss the content with your colleagues to ensure you all interpret them the same way.

External quality assurance

If your qualification is externally quality assured, a member of the relevant Awarding/Examining body will visit to ensure you are compliant with their requirements, and the requirements of regulatory bodies such as QCA and QAA.

Activity

Find out the name of the external verifier/moderator who has been allocated for your qualification. Keep a note of their contact details in case you need to get in touch to clarify anything.

Never be concerned about making contact with your external verifier/moderator. They are there to help ensure you assess the qualification correctly, and would not want you to do anything that contravenes the regulations. However, your organisation may prefer you to make contact through your internal verifier/moderator, to ensure they are aware of the advice and support given, and share this with the team.

The external verifier or moderator will:

- check that claims for certification are authentic, valid and supported by auditable records;
- complete a report and identify any relevant action;
- confirm that assessments are conducted by appropriately qualified staff;
- confirm that centres have carried out any previous corrective actions;
- ensure compliance with the approval criteria;
- ensure procedures are followed, including access to fair assessment and appeals;
- ensure that national standards are being consistently maintained;

- follow an audit trail through assessment and verification/moderation records;
- give advice and support regarding the interpretation of standards;
- observe assessment and verification/moderation;
- read minutes of meetings and check standardisation records;
- recommend sanctions for non compliance if requirements are not met;
- report any malpractice;
- sample assessment decisions to confirm that they are authentic and valid;
- talk to learners and others involved in the assessment process.

Prior to their visit, you will need to liaise with your internal verifier/moderator to ensure all the external requirements have been met, and that the requested sample of work is available. The external verifier/moderator may want to observe you with your learners, check your records, and sample your assessed work.

If you assess an NVQ, and the external verifier identifies non compliance, your organisation will receive a sanction at an appropriate level as stated in the Code of Practice (2006):

I   an action plan will be agreed; this is due to non compliance with the approval criteria but there is no threat to the integrity of assessment decisions;

2   removal of direct claims status for certification. Close scrutiny of the integrity of assessment decisions is required by the external verifier before any further certificates can be claimed;

3 (a) suspension of registration for further learners as there is a loss of the integrity of assessment decisions and a risk of invalid claims for certification; the external verifier will sample all claims for certification until the issues are resolved;

3 (b) suspension of certification for all learners, details as 3 (a);

4   withdrawal of approval for a particular qualification as there is an irretrievable breakdown in management and quality assurance; the Awarding/Examining body will arrange for learners to be transferred elsewhere;

5   withdrawal of approval for all qualifications within the organisation as there is an irretrievable breakdown in management and quality assurance of all NVQs offered by the organisation.

Example

The external verifier for your qualification has recently visited, and found that initial assessment activities were insufficient. This is a level one sanction; an action point was therefore given to ensure the organisation puts in procedures for initial assessment to take place, by an agreed date.

After a visit, your internal verifier/moderator should hold a meeting with the team to discuss any issues and action points. You should receive a copy of the minutes, and carry out any action points that have been allocated to you. The external verifier/moderator should then be informed when all the actions have been completed.

Always make sure you are assessing according to all the relevant regulations and guidelines, if you are in any doubt, talk to your internal verifier/moderator or person responsible for quality assurance within your organisation.

Summary

In this chapter you have learnt about:

- internal quality assurance;
- appeals, complaints and disputes;
- standardisation of practice;
- external quality assurance.

References and further information

Quality Assurance Agency (2006) *Code of Practice for the Assurance of Academic Quality and Standards in Higher Education.* Mansfield: QAA.
Qualifications and Curriculum Authority (2006) *NVQ Code of Practice.* London: QCA.
Wolf, A. (2008) Looking for the best result, in *Make the Grade,* summer 2008, Institute of Educational Assessors. www.ioea.org.uk

Websites

Learning and Skills Council – www.lsc.gov.uk
Ofqual – www.ofqual.gov.uk
Ofsted – www.ofsted.gov.uk
QAA – www.qaa.ac.uk
QCA – www.qca.org.uk
SSB and SSC details – www.ukstandards.org

6 EVALUATION

Introduction

In this chapter you will learn about:

- learner evaluation;

- programme evaluation;

- self evaluation;

- continuing professional development.

There are activities and examples to help you reflect on the above which will assist your understanding of evaluation, and continuing professional development CPD).

Chapter 7 contains useful pro-formas you may wish to use.

This chapter contributes towards the following: scope (S), knowledge (K) and practice (P) aspects of the professional standards (A–F domains) for teachers, tutors and trainers in the Lifelong Learning Sector.

AS4, AS5, AK1.1, AK2.1, AK4.2, AK4.3, AK5.1, AK7.3, AP3.1, AP4.2, AP4.3, AP5.1, AP5.2, AP7.2, AP7.3;
BK2.6, BP2.6, BP3.3, BP3.4 BP5.2;
CS1, CS3, CK4.1, CP1.1, CP3.4, CP4.1;
DS1, DS2, DS3, DK1.1, DK3.1, DK3.2, DP2.1, DP3.1, DP3.2;
ES4, ES5, EK2.1, EK2.2, EK2.4, EK4.1, EK4.2, EK5.1, EK5.3, EP1.1, EP2.4, EP3.1, EP4.1, EP4.2, EP5.1, EP5.2, EP5.5;
FS3, FK3.1, FK4.2.

This chapter contributes towards the following A1 and A2 standards:

A1.1m;
A1.2c, A1.2d, A1.2j;
A1.3e;
A1.4b, A1.4d.

A2.2h;
A2.3e.

Learner evaluation

Evaluation is not another term for *assessment*; evaluation is a way of obtaining *feedback* to improve your own performance, the support you give your learners, and to ensure the assessment processes used are effective, valid and reliable. Information gained from evaluations should lead to an improvement for learners, yourself and your organisation. Never assume everything is going well just because you think it is. Encouraging learners to talk to you about anything you can do to help them, or things you can change to support their learning, will help build a climate of trust and respect. Learners may be embarrassed to talk in front of their peers, but unless you know of any issues that may affect them, you can't fully support them.

As well as encouraging informal feedback and discussions, you can gain formal feedback from your learners by using surveys and questionnaires. Your organisation may have standard ones you are required to use, or you could design your own. Always build time into your session for this to take place, otherwise your learners will take away the questionnaire and may forget to return it.

When designing questionnaires, you need to be careful of the type of questions you are using, and consider why you are asking them. Don't just ask questions for the sake of issuing a questionnaire; consider what you really want to find out. When writing questions, gauge the language and level to suit your learners. Will your questions be closed, i.e. a question only requiring a *yes* or *no* answer, will they be multiple choice, enabling your learner to choose one or more responses to a question, or will they be open, leading to detailed responses?

Example

Was the assessment activity as you expected? YES/NO

This closed question would not help you to understand what it was that your learner expected, or even what their expectations were. This would be better phrased: **How did the assessment activity meet your expectations?** *This open question encourages your learner to answer in detail and gives you something to act on.*

If you would rather use questions with *yes/no* responses, you could ask a further question to enable your learner to elaborate on why they answered *yes* or *no*.

Example

Was the assessment activity as you expected? YES/NO
Why was this?

This enables your learner to expand on their response, and gives you more information.

If you use closed or multiple choice questions, you can add up how many responses you gained to give you *quantitative* data. Other responses will give you *qualitative* data. Quantitative data is useful for obtaining statistics, but will not give you much information to help you improve specific aspects of your programme. Although you can add up the responses quickly from quantitative data, qualitative data is more useful. You might find it best to use a mixture of open and closed questions. When designing questionnaires, use the KISS method – *Keep it Short and Simple*. Don't overcomplicate your questions, e.g. ask two questions in one sentence, or make the questionnaire so long that learners will not want to complete it. Inform your learners why you are asking them to complete the questionnaire and what the information will be used for. Always make sure you follow up their responses, and inform your learners of the results and actions to be taken, otherwise the evaluation process is meaningless.

Activity

Design a short questionnaire that you could use with your learners. This may be given to a group or an individual. Consider the types of questions you will ask, based upon the information you need. If possible, use it, analyse the results and recommend improvements to be made based on these.

Searching the internet will give you lots of ideas regarding questionnaire design.

You can also gain learner feedback after carrying out an assessment, for example, during a one to one conversation, or a group discussion. You may need to update or amend your learner's assessment plan, or revise the assessment process or any materials/resources used. You might find out that the method of assessment you have been using, for example projects and quizzes, is not challenging enough for your learner. They might prefer more formal methods such as a written test. Or perhaps a multiple choice test is not suitable for a learner with dyslexia, as they often mix up the *b* and *d* boxes on the answer sheet.

Some learners might not feel comfortable giving verbal feedback, and you may not have the opportunity to issue a questionnaire. A way to get around this could be to encourage anonymous feedback, perhaps by using a *feedback box*. This is similar to a suggestion box, but you could encourage *compliments* as well as *criticisms* or *complaints*. It doesn't have to be a box, it could be a large envelope pinned to a noticeboard, or a pigeonhole somewhere. If you do use this method, give your learners a summary of the information you have received and what you have acted upon. If learners take the time to give you feedback, you should also take the time to respond to it.

Programme evaluation

Whatever type of programme you are assessing, it is important to evaluate the process to ensure learning has been successful, and to inform future programme planning. It will also help you realise how effective you were and what you could improve in the future. It may help you identify any problem areas, enabling you to do things differently next time. Evaluating the programme will include analysing the results of questionnaires from your learners, as well as obtaining feedback from colleagues, management, employers, workplace supervisors, or inspectors and verifiers who may also be involved. Part of the quality assurance process will involve you being observed at some point.

Activity

If you have been observed lately, look at the feedback on the observation report. Was there anything identified that needed improving or changing; if so, have you done this?

If you haven't been observed, ask a colleague or your mentor to observe you, to gain constructive feedback.

Always make sure you do something with the feedback you receive, to help improve your assessment practice, and your learners' experiences in the future. You may not agree with some of the feedback. Don't take it personally, but learn from the experience of your observer. They may see things you didn't realise or appreciate. You could always ask if you could observe them, or another more experienced colleague, to help improve your practice.

If you are assessing employees in their place of work, you may like to obtain feedback from their employers to check that their newly acquired skills and knowledge have been put into practice successfully. If the employees are working towards a qualification, the employer may be paying for this and will want to know how they are progressing. If some of the employees did not achieve, the employer will want to know why. You would need to make an evaluation as to whether it was your planning and assessment methods or other factors that led to this. If you are giving feedback to others, always be tactful and diplomatic, and follow organisational procedures regarding confidentiality.

Example

Ravi had assessed Paul for a unit of the NVQ in Motor Vehicle Maintenance. After the assessment, Ravi didn't give Paul any feedback, but spoke directly to his employer about his progress. He informed the employer that Paul would never achieve the qualification and he didn't know why he had been employed in that trade in the first place.

In this instance, Ravi should have discussed the result of the assessment with Paul first: there could have been a legitimate reason as to why he hadn't performed well. If the employer wanted to be kept informed of Paul's progress, Ravi could have spoken to him in a more tactful way, explaining why Paul hadn't achieved, and planning a date for a further assessment. Learners need to be able to trust their assessors and to feel comfortable talking to them.

Your organisation may carry out an evaluation of your programme, perhaps to decide if it should be offered again in the future. They may make this decision based upon the number of learners recruited to the programme, their attendance patterns and whether they obtained a qualification at the end.

You may have to write a programme report which your organisation will use as a basis to make a decision about the future. This report may also include retention and achievement statistics. If the targets are not met, your programme may not be offered again. Some programmes may only be offered again if external funding can be obtained.

Activity

Find out how the programmes you assess are funded. Does this come from the local Learning and Skills Council (LSC), Local Education Authority (LEA), do your learners or their employers pay, do they receive a grant, or does your organisation fund it?

Knowing how your programme is funded will help you realise the constraints and pressures your learners and your organisation may be under. If your learners do not achieve within the designated time period, you may need to carry out further assessments which will impact on the overall success rates, the funding received, and also add further work for yourself as you may need to carry out more assessments.

If you assess a programme which requires grades to be given to learners, you will need to analyse data regarding their achievements. The grades could be expressed as:

- 1, 2, 3, 4, 5;
- A, B, C, D, E;
- competent/not yet competent;
- distinction, credit, pass, fail;
- pass, refer, fail;
- percentages;
- satisfactory, good, outstanding.

Once you have analysed your data, you will need to consider what has contributed towards them. For example, if you had a group of 30 learners who all achieved an A grade, was this due to your excellent teaching and assessing, the skills and knowledge of your learners, or by being too lenient with your grades when marking? If you had a group of 15 learners who all failed an assignment, you could ask yourself the same questions. However, it could be that the assignment questions were worded in a confusing way, or you had given the assignment too early in the programme. If most of your group averaged a grade of 50%, whereas a colleague's group's averaged 80%, was this because you had given your learners misleading or ambiguous information relating to that topic? Asking yourself these questions will help you ascertain if you are producing assessments that are fit for purpose, and if not, you will need to do something about it, for example, amending your teaching or assessment methods, or rewording questions.

It is important to attend team meetings to keep up to date with any changes or developments. If you can't attend a meeting for any reason, make sure you obtain the minutes, and read and act upon any recommendations.

Your organisation might employ new assessors and you may be asked to mentor and support them. They should be given an induction to the assessment policy and procedures, all relevant paperwork and systems, the Awarding/Examining body requirements as well as your organisational requirements. If assessors are leaving, there should be a system of succession planning, to allow time for a successful handover, and any relevant training to take place. Usually, the Awarding/Examining body will need to be informed of any new staff.

You may need to evaluate the resources you use, for example handouts, to ensure they are inclusive, promote equality and engage with diversity. You will also need to evaluate whether the assessment types and methods you used were successful. You will need to ensure the activities you used to assess knowledge, skills and attitudes were valid and reliable, and that you only assessed the criteria you were meant to assess. You will need to ask yourself if you assessed fairly, or if you had a favourite learner to whom you gave more attention, or were lenient with for any reason.

Example

Lorraine had taken a group of 24 learners for a programme which had marking criteria of pass, refer and fail for three assignments. The qualification was not externally accredited, i.e. the organisation issued their own certificates, but marking guidance had been agreed by the programme team. Lorraine had one particular learner who had problems at home, and already had two assignments referred. Both assignments had been resubmitted by the learner who subsequently achieved a pass, only due to Lorraine's extra support. The third assignment should have been another refer, but Lorraine gave a pass, as she did not want to demoralise her learner any more, nor be seen to give him more support.

In this instance, Lorraine had not been fair to the group, as she had given extra support to one particular learner. If all the learners had struggled, she could evaluate why this was: perhaps the assignment instructions were not clear. She should not have given a grade of *pass* if it should have been *refer*, as this is an invalid result. It is also not a reliable result as all the learners' responses are not being assessed consistently. However, there will be instances when a particular learner may require extra support, due to their individual needs.

You will also need to ensure you are giving feedback which is developmental to your learner, advising and guiding them where and how they can improve and not giving them support to the extent that their work becomes partly yours.

Standardising your practice with other assessors, verification and moderation will help ensure you are assessing fairly and consistently.

Self evaluation

Self evaluation is about assessing your own practice. You need to evaluate yourself, to ensure you are carrying out your role effectively. When evaluating your own practice, you need to consider *how* your own behaviour has impacted upon your learners and *what* you could do to improve as an assessor.

Activity

Think about the last assessment activity you carried out. Did it go as planned? If not, why not? What could you do to put this right?

It could be that you didn't have enough time to plan the assessment in advance, therefore not giving enough information to your learners. Or you might have rushed the assessment due to time constraints, or couldn't complete the paper-work fully. After each assessment activity you carry out, evaluate how you feel it went, what was good about it and what could be improved.

A straightforward method of reflection is to have the *experience*, then *describe it, analyse it* and *revise it* (EDAR). This method should help you think about what has happened and then consider ways of changing and/or improving it.

Experience → *Describe* → *Analyse* → *Revise*

EDAR (Gravells 2008)

- *Experience* – a significant event or incident you would like to change or improve.

- *Describe* – aspects such as *who* was involved, *what* happened, *when* it happened and *where* it happened.

- *Analyse* – consider the experience deeper and ask yourself *how* it happened and *why* it happened.

- *Revise* – think about *how* you would do it differently if it happened again and then try this out if you have the opportunity.

A way of getting in the habit of reflective practice is to complete an ongoing journal; however, try not to write it like a diary with a description of events, but use EDAR to reflect upon the event.

Activity

Use the reflective learning journal pro-forma in the appendices to reflect upon your last assessment activity, using EDAR to help you. Did you have any issues or problems during the assessment process? If you did, what could you do to stop this happening again?

You may see your own skills developing, for example giving effective, developmental and constructive feedback.

Reflection should become a habit. If you are not able to write a reflective journal, mentally run through the EDAR points in your head when you have time. As you become more experienced at reflective practice, you will progress from thoughts of *I should have let my learner realise their own mistake before stepping in* to aspects of more significance to your professional role as an assessor. You may realise you need further training or support in some areas before feeling confident to make changes.

Keeping a reflective learning journal will help you plan aspects for your continuing professional development (CPD).

Continuing professional development

Initial professional development (IPD) begins if you are not already qualified or are currently working towards a qualification; continuing professional development (CPD) should be carried out regularly, to maintain your occupational competence.

As a professional, you need to continually update your skills and knowledge. This knowledge relates not only to your subject specialism, but assessment methods, the types of learners you will be assessing, and relevant organisational and national policies. CPD can be formal or informal, planned well in advance or be opportunistic, but it should have a real impact upon your job role and lead to an improvement in your practice as an assessor.

CPD is more than just attending events; it is also using critical reflection regarding your experiences which result in your development as an assessor. Shadowing colleagues, for example, observing how they assess, joining professional associations, and internet research will all help your development.

> Reflection is not simply something that you should do to meet the criteria once a development activity has been completed; it is integral to the whole process of professional growth.
>
> Hitching (2008:13)

You can update your CPD via the IfL website (www.ifl.ac.uk); by now you should have registered as a member and you will have access to a wealth of information regarding ways to maintain your CPD.

When planning your CPD, it is a good idea to complete a *personal development plan*. This enables you to consider your development needs and the best way to achieve them which should relate directly to your job role or subject specialism.

Activity

Consider what CPD you feel is relevant, for example, improving your literacy or numeracy skills. Use the personal development plan pro-forma in Chapter 7 to formalise your requirements.

Having the support of your organisation will help you decide what is relevant to your development as an assessor, and your job role.

You will probably partake in an appraisal system at your organisation. This is a valuable opportunity to discuss your learning and any training or support you may need in the future. Always keep a copy of any documentation relating to your training and CPD, as you may need to provide this to funding, Awarding/Examining or regulatory bodies if requested.

The practice of assessment has been recognised as a professional activity by the granting of Chartered Status to the Institute of Educational Assessors (CIEA). Their aim is to improve the quality of assessment in schools and colleges by working with educational assessors to develop their knowledge, understanding and capability in all aspects of educational testing and assessment. You can access their standards by visiting their website (www.ciea.org.uk).

Reflecting upon your own assessment practice, taking account of feedback from learners and colleagues, evaluating your practice and maintaining your professional development, will enable you to become a more effective assessor.

Summary

In this chapter you have learnt about:

- learner evaluation;

- programme evaluation;

- self evaluation;

- continuing professional development.

References and further information

Hitching, J. (2008) *Maintaining Your Licence to Practise*. Exeter: Learning Matters.
Tummons, J. (2007) *Assessing Learning in the Lifelong Learning Sector*. Exeter: Learning Matters.
Wallace, S. and Gravells, J. (2007) *Mentoring*. Exeter: Learning Matters.

Websites

Chartered Institute of Educational Assessors – www.ciea.org.uk
Institute for Learning – www.lfl.ac.uk
Learning and Skills Council – www.lsc.gov.uk
Lifelong Learning UK – www.lluk.org.uk
Post Compulsory Education & Training Network – www.pcet.net

This chapter contains sample documents referred to within the previous chapters, which you may like to use in preparation for, or as part of, your assessment role. They are examples only, and can be adapted to suit your own requirements. If you are currently assessing, your organisation will already have certain documents they will require you to use, which may differ from these.

The documents are also available from the publisher's website: www.learning matters.co.uk.

- Initial assessment record

- Assessment plan and review

- Skills and knowledge report

- Feedback and action plan

- Assessment tracking sheet

- Standardisation record

- Personal development plan

- Continuing professional development record

- Reflective learning journal

Initial assessment record

Name: **Date:**

Programme/Qualification: **Venue:**

What relevant experience do you have?		
What relevant qualifications do you have?		
Have you completed a learning styles questionnaire? If YES, what is your preferred style of learning?	YES/NO	
Do you have any particular learning needs or special requirements? If YES, please state, or talk to your assessor in confidence.	YES/NO	
Are you confident at using a computer? If YES, what experience or qualifications do you have?	YES/NO	*Skills scan results:* ICT:
Do you feel you have a good command of written/ spoken English?	YES/NO	*Skills scan results:* Literacy:
Do you feel your numeracy skills need improving?	YES/NO	*Skills scan results:* Numeracy:
Why have you decided to take this programme/ qualification (*continue overleaf*)		

An individual assessment plan should now be agreed.

Signed (assessor):   Signed (learner):

Assessment plan and review

Learner: **Assessor:**

Qualification and level: **Registration number:**

Date commenced: **Expected completion date:**

Date	Aspect of qualification (unit/ element/ criteria etc)	Date achieved	Assessment details **Planning** – methods of assessment, activities and SMART targets **Review** – revisions to plan, achievements and issues discussed	Target/ review date	Agreed by (assessor and learner to sign)

This document is an ongoing record of learner progress.

Separate records must be completed for the assessment of skills and knowledge, and feedback and action.

Countersignature and date (if required):

Skills and knowledge report

Learner: **Assessor:**

Qualification: **Level:**

Date assessed: **Date feedback given:**

Aspect of qualification assessed (unit/element/ criteria etc) **formative/summative**	**Skills** – observation of performance: state what was observed and how the aspects were achieved in relation to the qualification **Knowledge** – note questions and responses, results of APL/tests & activities, professional discussion points etc

Assessment was conducted under the specified conditions or context of the qualification

Assessment decision: valid ☐ authentic ☐ current ☐ sufficient ☐ reliable ☐
competent/not yet competent
further action required? YES/NO
feedback and action plan completed? YES/NO

Signed (assessor):   Signed (learner):

Countersignature and date (if required):

Feedback and action plan

Learner: **Assessor:**

Qualification: **Level:**

Aspect of qualification assessed	Feedback	Action required (assessment plan to be updated)	Target date

Signed (assessor):   Date:

Signed (learner):   Date:

Countersignature and date (if required):

Assessment tracking sheet

Assessor:

Qualification and level:

Learners:

Aspect of
qualification:

Enter date and grade achieved for each aspect or unit of the qualification

Standardisation record

Learner:			Registration no:	
Qualification:			Level:	
Standardising assessor:			Original assessor:	
Aspect/s standardised:				
Checklist	Yes	No	Action required	
Is there an agreed appropriate assessment/action plan with SMART targets?				
Are the assessment methods appropriate and sufficient? Which methods were used?				
Does the evidence meet ALL the required criteria?				
Does the evidence meet VACSR?				
Is there an assessment feedback record (adequate and developmental)?				
Do you agree with the assessment decision?				
Are all relevant documents signed and dated (including countersignatures if applicable)?				
Has the unit declaration been signed and dated (if applicable)?				
Are original assessment records stored separately from the learner's work?				
Comments from original assessor:				

(A1 candidates must ensure two pieces of evidence from each of their two candidates are standardised.)

Signed (standardising assessor):   **Date:**

Signed (original assessor):   **Date:**

Key: SMART: specific, measureable, achievable, realistic, time bound
       VACSR: valid, authentic, current, sufficient, reliable

Personal development plan

Name:

Organisation:

Timescale	Aims	Costs involved/ organisational support	Start date	Review date	Completion date CPD record to be updated
Short term					
Medium term					
Long term					

Continuing professional development record

Name:

Organisation:

IfL number:

Date	Activity	Venue	Duration	Justification towards assessment role/ subject specialism	Further training needs	Evidence Ref Number e.g. personal reflections, notes, certificates etc

Reflective learning journal

Name: **Date:**

Experience *significant event or incident*	
Describe *who, what, when, where*	
Analyse *why, how (impact on teaching and learning)*	
Revise *changes and/or improvements required*	

UNIT TITLE: Principles and practice of assessment level 3 (three credits)

Learning outcomes The learner can:	Assessment criteria The learner will:
1 Understand key concepts and principles of assessment	1.1 Identify and define the key concepts and principles of assessment
2 Understand and use different types of assessment	2.1 Explain and demonstrate how different types of assessment can be used effectively to meet the individual needs of learners
3 Understand the strengths and limitations of a range of assessment methods, including, as appropriate, those which exploit new and emerging technologies	3.1 Identify the strengths and limitations of a range of assessment methods with reference to the needs of particular learners and key concepts and principles of assessment 3.2 Use a range of assessment methods appropriately to ensure that learners produce assessment evidence that is valid, authentic, current, sufficient and reliable 3.3 Explain how peer and self-assessment can be used to promote learner involvement and personal responsibility in the assessment of their learning
4 Understand the role of feedback and questioning in the assessment of learning	4.1 Explain how feedback and questioning contributes to the assessment process 4.2 Use feedback and questioning effectively in the assessment of learning
5 Understand how to monitor, assess, record and report learner progress and achievement to meet the requirements of the learning programme and the organisation	5.1 Specify the assessment requirements and related procedures of a particular learning programme 5.2 Conduct and record assessments which meet the requirements of the learning programme and the organisation including, where appropriate, the requirements of external bodies 5.3 Communicate relevant assessment information to those with a legitimate interest in learner achievement
6 Understand how to evaluate the effectiveness of own practice	6.1 Reflect on the effectiveness of own practice taking account of the views of learners

UNIT TITLE: Principles and practice of assessment level 4 (three credits)

Learning outcomes: The learner will:	Assessment criteria The learner can:
1 Understand key concepts and principles of assessment	1.1 Summarise the key concepts and principles of assessment
2 Understand and use different types of assessment	2.1 Discuss and demonstrate how different types of assessment can be used effectively to meet the individual needs of learners
3 Understand the strengths and limitations of a range of assessment methods, including, as appropriate, those which exploit new and emerging technologies	3.1 Evaluate a range of assessment methods with reference to the needs of particular learners and key concepts and principles of assessment 3.2 Use a range of assessment methods appropriately to ensure that learners produce assessment evidence that is valid, authentic, current, sufficient and reliable 3.3 Justify the use of peer and self-assessment to promote learner involvement and personal responsibility in the assessment of their learning
4 Understand the role of feedback and questioning in the assessment of learning	4.1 Analyse how feedback and questioning contributes to the assessment process 4.2 Use feedback and questioning effectively in the assessment of learning
5 Understand how to monitor, assess, record and report learner progress and achievement to meet the requirements of the learning programme and the organisation	5.1 Review the assessment requirements and related procedures of a particular learning programme 5.2 Conduct and record assessments which meet the requirements of the learning programme and the organisation including, where appropriate, the requirements of external bodies 5.3 Communicate relevant assessment information to those with a legitimate interest in learner achievement
6 Understand how to evaluate the effectiveness of own practice	6.1 Evaluate the effectiveness of own practice taking account of the views of learners

The *New overarching professional standards for teachers, tutors and trainers in the life-long learning sector* (LLUK 2007) can be accessed at: www.lluk.org./documents/professional_standards_for_itts_020107.pdf.

Or by using the shortcut: http://tinyurl.com/5mmg9s.

A1 – Assess candidates using a range of methods

A1.1: Develop plans for assessing competence with candidates

Performance criteria

- Develop and agree an assessment plan with candidates.

- Check that all candidates understand the assessment process involved, the support available to them and the complaints and appeals procedure.

- Agree fair, safe, valid and reliable assessment methods.

- Identify appropriate and cost-effective opportunities for assessing performance.

- Plan for using different types of evidence.

- Identify how the past experiences and achievements of candidates will contribute to the assessment process.

- Identify and agree any special arrangements needed to make sure the assessment process is fair.

- Identify how other people will contribute to assessments and what support they may need.

- Identify how to protect confidentiality and agree arrangements to deal with sensitive issues.

- Agree how you will handle any difficulties or disputes during the assessment.

- Agree when assessment will take place with candidates and the other people involved.

- Agree arrangements with candidates for reviewing their progress against the assessment plan.

- Review and update assessment plans to take account of what the candidates have achieved.

A1.2: Judge evidence against criteria to make assessment decisions
Performance criteria

- Use the agreed assessment methods to assess competence in appropriate situations.

- Use the past experiences and achievements of candidates as part of the assessment of their current competence.

- Ensure that the evidence comes from the candidates' own work.

- Make safe, fair, valid and reliable decisions about the competence of candidates, only on the agreed standard.

- Collect evidence from the other people involved in the assessment process.

- Apply any agreed special arrangements to make sure the assessment is fair.

- Base your decisions on all the relevant evidence of candidates' performance and knowledge. Take this evidence from as many places as possible.

- Explain and resolve any inconsistencies in the evidence.

- Make a record of the outcomes of assessments by using the agreed recording system.

- Speak to the appropriate person if you and the candidate cannot agree on your assessment of their performance.

A1.3: Provide feedback and support to candidates on assessment decisions
Performance criteria

- Give candidates feedback at an appropriate time and place.

- Give candidates feedback in a constructive and encouraging way, which meets their needs and is appropriate to their level of confidence.

- Clearly explain your assessment decisions on whether candidates' evidence of competence is good enough.

- Give candidates advice when they cannot prove their competence and on how they can develop the necessary skills or provide more evidence.

- Encourage candidates to get advice on your assessment decisions.

- Identify and agree the next steps in the assessment process and how candidates will achieve these.

- Follow the agreed complaints and appeals procedures if candidates disagree with your assessment decisions.

A1.4: Contribute to the internal quality assurance process

Performance criteria

● Ensure your assessment records are accurate and up to date, and provide an audit trail of evidence.

● Contribute to standardisation arrangements so that your assessment decisions are in line with others.

● Give accurate and timely information on assessments.

● Contribute to the agreed quality assurance process.

A2 – Assess candidates' performance through observation

A 2.1: Agree and review plans for assessing candidates' performance

Performance criteria

- Identify the best situations when you can assess performance.

- Use evidence that takes place in the workplace and ask relevant questions.

- Choose opportunities for assessment which disrupt normal work as little as possible.

- Choose opportunities for assessment which provide access to a valid, safe, reliable and fair assessment.

- Explain the options open to the candidates clearly and constructively if somebody disagrees with the proposed assessment plan.

- Discuss and agree the proposed assessment plan with the candidates and other people who may be affected.

- Review and update plans at agreed times to take account of candidates' progress.

A2.2: Assess candidates' performance against the agreed standards

Performance criteria

- Explain to candidates how the assessment of their work will take account of their needs.

- Watch candidates in a safe environment.

- Only use the agreed criteria when assessing the evidence.

- Assess evidence fairly against the agreed criteria.

- Identify and assess any other evidence that is relevant to the standards.

- Check that the evidence has come from each candidate's own work.

- Watch candidates without interfering with their work.

- Speak to the appropriate person if you or a candidate has any difficulties.

- Give candidates feedback after you have watched them in the workplace.

A2.3: Assess candidates' knowledge against the agreed standard
Performance criteria

- Identify which areas of candidates' knowledge have been covered by watching them in the workplace.

- Collect evidence of knowledge that has not been covered by watching the candidates in the workplace.

- Use valid methods to assess candidates' knowledge.

- Ask clear questions which do not 'lead' candidates.

- Speak to the appropriate person if you or a candidate has any difficulties.

- Give candidates feedback after you have asked them questions.

A2.4: Make an assessment decision and provide feedback
Performance criteria

- Base your assessment decision on all the relevant evidence.

- Give candidates clear and constructive feedback, which meets their needs after you have given them your assessment.

- Encourage candidates to ask for advice on your assessment decision.

- Make an accurate record of your assessment decisions.

- Pass on records that are accurate and easy to read to the next stage of the process.

- Follow the agreed complaints and appeals procedures if candidates do not agree with your assessment decisions.

APPENDIX 4 LIST OF ABBREVIATIONS AND ACRONYMS

AB – Awarding Body

ACL - Adult and Community Learning

APEL – Accreditation of Prior Experience and Learning

APL – Accreditation of Prior Learning

ASSC – Alliance of Sector Skills Councils

ATLS – Associate Teacher Learning and Skills

CCEA – Council for the Curriculum, Examinations and Assessment

CEHR – Commission for Equality and Human Rights

CIEA – Chartered Institute of Educational Assessors

CPD – Continuing Professional Development

CTLLS – Certificate in Teaching in the Lifelong Learning Sector

DCFS – Department for Children, Families and Schools

DDA – Disability Discrimination Act

DIUS – Department for Innovation, Universities and Skills

DTLLS – Diploma in Teaching in the Lifelong Learning Sector

ESOL – English for Speakers of Other Languages

GCSE – General Certificate of Secondary Education

HEI – Higher Education Institute

HSE – Health and Safety Executive

ICT – Information Communication Technology

IfL – Institute for Learning

ILP – Individual Learning Plan

IPD – Initial Professional Development

ITT– Initial Teacher Training

LEA – Local Education Authority

LLN – Language, Literacy, Numeracy

LLUK – Lifelong Learning UK

LSC – Learning and Skills Council

LSN – Learning and Skills Network

NIACE – National Institute of Adult Continuing Education

NOS – National Occupational Standards

NVQ – National Vocational Qualification

Ofqual – Office of the Qualifications and Examinations Regulator

OfSTED – Office for Standards in Education, Children's Services and Skills

PCET – Post Compulsory Education and Training

PTLLS – Preparing to Teach in the Lifelong Learning Sector

QAA – Quality Assurance Agency

QCA - Qualifications and Curriculum Authority

QCF – Qualification and Credit Framework

QIA – Quality Improvement Agency

QTLS – Qualified Teacher Learning and Skills

RARPA – Recognition and Recording of Progress and Achievement

RWE – Realistic Working Environment

SMART – Specific, Measurable, Achievable, Realistic and Time bound

SQA – Scottish Qualifications Authority

SSB - Standards Setting Bodies

SSC – Sector Skills Council

SVQ - Scottish Vocational Qualification

SVUK – Standards Verification UK

VACSR – Valid, Authentic, Current, Sufficient, Reliable

VARK – Visual, Aural, Read/Write, Kinaesthetic

VDU – Visual Display Unit

VLE – Virtual Learning Environment

WBL - Work Based Learning

WWWWWH – Who, What, When, Where, Why and How

APPENDIX 5 ASSESSOR CHECKLIST

☐ Do I need to achieve the Assessor Unit A1 or A2 to assess NVQs? If so, do I know who will countersign my decisions until I am qualified?

☐ Do I need to participate in any CPD?

☐ Do I have a copy of the qualification handbook and assessment strategy?

☐ Do I understand QCA/QAA and Awarding/Examining body requirements for the qualification?

☐ Do I attend regular team meetings?

☐ Do I have the opportunity to standardise my practice with other assessors?

☐ Does my internal verifier/moderator or manager need to observe my practice?

☐ Do I know who my external verifier/moderator is?

☐ Have all my learners been registered with the Awarding/Examining body?

☐ Am I familiar with the organisation's policies and procedures?

☐ Do I have an overall assessment tracking sheet for my group?

☐ Do I need to carry out initial assessments with my learners?

☐ Have I completed individual assessment plans with each learner, with suitable dates, times and assessment methods, taking into account any special assessment requirements and health and safety aspects? Does the learner have a copy?

☐ Do I need to liaise with anyone else, for example workplace supervisors?

☐ Can I differentiate my activities to suit all my learners?

☐ Can I utilise new and emerging technologies?

☐ Do I need to produce a marking scheme with expected responses?

☐ Do I need to complete any specific records whilst assessing performance or knowledge?

☐ Did the evidence I assessed meet standards of validity, authenticity, currency, sufficiency and reliability?

☐ Do I feel confident at making assessment decisions?

☐ After each assessment, have I completed the feedback record and given a copy to the learner?

☐ Was my feedback positive and developmental?

☐ Do I need to review the learner's assessment plan for future or additional assessments?

☐ Do I keep copies of records in accordance with the Awarding/Examining body requirements?

☐ Do I need to sign a unit declaration for NVQs?

☐ Do I know what to do if a learner appeals against my decision?

INDEX

Note: the letter 's' after a page number refers to a sample document/pro-forma.

with learners 17–18, 30, 31, 32–3, 36
non-verbal communication 17, 60, 61
with parents/guardians/carers 16, 17, 66
with persons involved in learning and
   assessment 15, 16–17, 18, 19, 31, 83
professionalism 15, 16–19
and reviewing progress 63
verbal 17, 59, 60, 61, 81, 82
written communication 17–18, 26, 47,
   59–60
   see also discussions; feedback; oral
   questions; professional discussions
communication skills 17–18
competence-based assessment 25, 26, 28,
   45, 46
   see also NVQs (National Vocational
   Qualifications); observations; SVQs
   (Scottish Vocational Qualifications);
   witness testimonies
complaints see appeals, complaints and
   disputes
concepts and principles of assessment
   assessment cycle 8–10
   communicating with others 15, 16–19
   concepts 7–8
   roles and responsibilities 10–16
confidence levels 13, 46, 50, 59, 61
confidentiality
   and appeals, complaints and disputes 75
   and feedback 83
   and methods of assessment 45, 46, 49
   and recording progress 67
   and reviewing progress 63, 64
conflicts of interest 32
constructive feedback
   advantages 61
   and decision making 55
   and motivating learners 7, 14, 60, 61
   and negative feedback 7, 55, 59, 60, 62
   and reviewing progress 63
continuing professional development 3,
   72, 87–8, 97s
continuing professional development
   record 97s
copies for learners 64, 66, 68
copying 44, 47, 68, 69
copyright 13, 69
Copyright, Designs and Patents Act (1988)
   69
correcting errors 59, 60
creativity 39

credits (QCF) 2–3
criterion referencing 28
critical thinking skills 28, 47
CTLLS (Certificate in Teaching in the
   Lifelong Learning Sector) 3
culture, equality and diversity 50, 51
currency 42, 46, 53–4, 92s, 95s

data protection 13, 67
Data Protection Act (1998) 67
dating
   of records 64, 68, 90–3s, 95
   of work submitted 68, 69
deaf learners 34, 52
debates 43, 46, 48, 49
decision making in assessment 8, 9, 54–6,
   83
demonstrating tasks 12
Department for Education, Children's
   Services and Skills 38–9
describe, in EDAR 86, 87, 98s
developmental feedback 59, 60, 61, 62, 63,
   85
developmental notes 59
diagnostic assessment 21–3, 28, 90s
diaries/journals 24, 29, 45, 86–7, 98s
diplomas (QCF) 2, 3
direct assessment 29
   see also NVQs (national vocational
   qualifications)
Disability Discrimination Act (1995) 52–3
disabled learners 34, 35, 51, 52–3
disagreements see appeals, complaints and
   disputes
disclosure, by learners 53, 64
discussions
   and evaluation 81, 82
   and feedback 60, 61
   as method of assessment 24, 43, 46, 48,
   49
   professional discussions 46, 66, 92s
   and quality assurance 79
   and reviewing progress 62, 65
disputes see appeals, complaints and
   disputes
dissertations/reports/research 47, 56
diversity see equality and diversity
do 25, 26, 28
   see also actions
documents 9, 51–2, 77
double marking 15, 76

records of assessment *see* assessment
records
Reece, I. 7
referrals, for expert advice 16, 64
referrals, for reassessment 54, 85
reflection 28, 29, 86–7, 98s
reflective learning journal 29, 86–7, 98s
registration 31, 66
registration, suspension of 78
regulations
 and approval when adapting to learners'
 needs 35, 51
 health and safety 12–13
 language, literacy, numeracy, ICT skills
 59
 quality assurance 77–9
 retakes 54
 teacher status 3
regulatory bodies 66, 74
reliability 24, 27–8, 38, 39, 43, 53–4, 81,
 85, 92s, 95s
religion, and equality 51
report, of programme evaluation 83
reports/research/dissertations 47, 56
research skills 47
resources
 adapting to learners' needs 34, 35, 51,
 52, 53
 evaluation 85
 methods of assessment 39
retakes 54
retention statistics 67, 84
reviewing progress
 in assessment cycle 8, 9
 described 62–5
 in feedback sessions 59
 recording progress 31, 62, 63, 64, 66,
 70, 91s
revise, in EDAR 86, 87, 98s
right-handed students, and one-to-one
 demonstrating tasks 12
risk assessment 12–13, 41
role plays 24, 48

safe assessment environments 49, 65
safety, of records 62, 67
sample documentation/pro-formas 89,
 90–8s
sanctions for non compliance with NVQ
 regulations 76, 78
scenarios/case studies 42, 55
schemes of work 63, 64, 67

scope 26
 see also professional teaching standards
Scottish Qualifications Authority (SQA) 4
screening 21, 30
second opinions 55
Sector Skills Councils (SSCs) 4, 8, 74
secure assessment environments 49, 65
security, of records 62, 67
self-actualisation 65
self-assessment 29, 33, 45, 48, 67, 70
self-assessment reports 67
self-confidence levels 13, 46, 50, 59, 61
self-esteem 65
self-evaluation 86–7, 98s
sensitive issues 16, 63, 64
session plans 63, 64, 67
sexual orientation, and equality 51
short answers 47
short term assessment planning 32–3
sight-impaired learners 34, 35, 52
signatures
 on receiving decision and feedback 56
 on records 68, 90–3s, 95
 on reviewing progress 62, 64
 on work submitted 56, 68, 69
Simpson, S. 1, 26, 54
simulation 27, 48
skills
 in Bloom's Taxonomy of Educational
 Objectives 25, 26
 evaluation 85
 and methods of assessment 44, 45, 47
 and recording progress 66, 92s
 see also critical thinking skills; functional
 skills; ICT (information
 communication technology) skills;
 language skills; listening skills; literacy
 skills; numeracy skills; questioning
 skills; transferable skills
skills and knowledge report 66, 92s
skills scans 21–3, 28, 90s
SMART (specific, measurable, achievable,
 realistic, time bound)
 assessment planning 32, 33, 34, 91s
 methods of assessment 39
 recording progress 91s, 95s
 reviewing progress 64
 see also achievements of learners; time
 factors; specific feedback
special needs 34–5, 41, 51–3, 90s
specialist support 16, 34, 35, 64
specific feedback 59, 60, 62

THOR

God of Thunder Reborn

JASON AARON
WRITER

#1–4

MIKE DEL MUNDO
ARTIST

MARCO D'ALFONSO
COLOR ASSISTS, #1 & #3-4

CHRISTIAN WARD
"THE GRACE OF THOR" ARTIST

#5–6

CHRISTIAN WARD
ARTIST

ESAD RIBIĆ
COVER ART

VC's JOE SABINO
LETTERER

MIKE DEL MUNDO
COVER ART

SARAH BRUNSTAD
ASSOCIATE EDITOR

WIL MOSS
EDITOR

TOM BREVOORT
EXECUTIVE EDITOR

THOR CREATED BY
STAN LEE, LARRY LIEBER & JACK KIRBY

COLLECTION EDITOR: JENNIFER GRÜNWALD • ASSISTANT EDITOR: CAITLIN O'CONNELL
ASSOCIATE MANAGING EDITOR: KATERI WOODY • EDITOR, SPECIAL PROJECTS: MARK D. BEAZLEY
VP PRODUCTION & SPECIAL PROJECTS: JEFF YOUNGQUIST • SVP PRINT, SALES & MARKETING: DAVID GABRIEL
BOOK DESIGNER: JAY BOWEN

EDITOR IN CHIEF: C.B. CEBULSKI • CHIEF CREATIVE OFFICER: JOE QUESADA
PRESIDENT: DAN BUCKLEY • EXECUTIVE PRODUCER: ALAN FINE

THOR VOL. 1: GOD OF THUNDER REBORN. Contains material originally published in magazine form as THOR #1-6. First printing 2018. ISBN 978-1-302-91289-5. Published by MARVEL WORLDWIDE, INC., a subsidiary of MARVEL ENTERTAINMENT, LLC. OFFICE OF PUBLICATION: 135 West 50th Street, New York, NY 10020. **Printed in Canada.** DAN BUCKLEY, President, Marvel Entertainment; JOHN NEE, Publisher; JOE QUESADA, Chief Creative Officer; TOM BREVOORT, SVP of Publishing; DAVID BOGART, SVP of Business Affairs & Operations, Publishing & Partnership; DAVID GABRIEL, SVP of Sales & Marketing, Publishing; JEFF YOUNGQUIST, VP of Production & Special Projects; DAN CARR, Executive Director of Publishing Technology; ALEX MORALES, Director of Publishing Operations; DAN EDINGTON, Managing Editor; SUSAN CRESPI, Production Manager; STAN LEE, Chairman Emeritus. For information regarding advertising in Marvel Comics or on Marvel.com, please contact Vit DeBellis, Custom Solutions & Integrated Advertising Manager, at vdebellis@marvel.com. For Marvel subscription inquiries, please call 888-511-5480. **Manufactured between 10/26/2018 and 11/27/2018 by SOLISCO PRINTERS, SCOTT, QC, CANADA.**

10 9 8 7 6 5 4 3 2 1

"GOD OF THUNDER REBORN"

PREVIOUSLY IN

THOR

THOR IS BACK. WHILE STILL UNWORTHY OF LIFTING HIS
HAMMER, MJOLNIR, HE IS ONCE MORE THE GOD OF THUNDER.

JUST IN TIME, TOO. FOR THE CITY OF ASGARDIA HAS BEEN
DESTROYED, JANE FOSTER IS STILL BATTLING CANCER
AND ALL-FATHER ODIN IS BUSY TRYING TO RESTORE OLD
ASGARD TO ITS FORMER GLORY. SO IT'S UP TO THOR TO STOP
MALEKITH'S ATTEMPT TO CONQUER ALL OF THE TEN REALMS.
BUT WITH THE RAINBOW BRIDGE SHATTERED, HE HAS NO
WAY OF TAKING THE FIGHT TO THE DARK ELF KING.

THOR NEEDN'T WORRY, HOWEVER—SOON THE WAR OF
THE REALMS WILL BE COMING TO EARTH...

"THE GRACE OF THOR"

IN THE FAR FUTURE, ALL-FATHER THOR AND HIS THREE
GRANDDAUGHTERS RESPARKED LIFE ON PLANET EARTH
AFTER MILLENNIA HAD LEFT IT BARREN. THE FIRST NEW
HUMANS WERE NAMED "STEVE" AND "JANE" AND GIVEN
FREE REIN OVER THE NEW MIDGARD.

INWORTHINESS. THE DISCIPLES OF THANOS. THE MANGOG AND THE DESTRUCTION OF ASGARDIA. THE FALL OF THE NEW THOR. THE DEATH OF MJOLNIR.

AND NOW I SUPPOSE YOU CAN ADD "CORNERED BY A CULT OF DEMON-WORSHIPING CANNIBALS" TO THE LIST.

UT EVEN WITH MY ENCHANTED AMMER LOST FOREVER IN THE UN, THE GOD OF THUNDER'S ORK IS NEVER DONE.

END OF THE ROAD, THIEF!

NO HAMMER, NO FLYING AWAY FOR YOU, THUNDER FOOL.

HEH. NOT A GOOD DAY TO BE A FALSE GOD IN THE TEMPLE OF THE ONE TRUE RAGE-FATHER, IS IT?

THERE MUST ALWAYS BE A THOR, OR SO I HAVE BEEN TOLD. VERILY, I DOTH HEARTILY AGREE.

AYE. 'TIS INDEED MOST UNFORTUNATE.

AS OVER THE CENTURIES, I HAVE LEARNED TO QUITE ENJOY BEING ME.

UNFORTUNATE FOR ALL OF YOU.

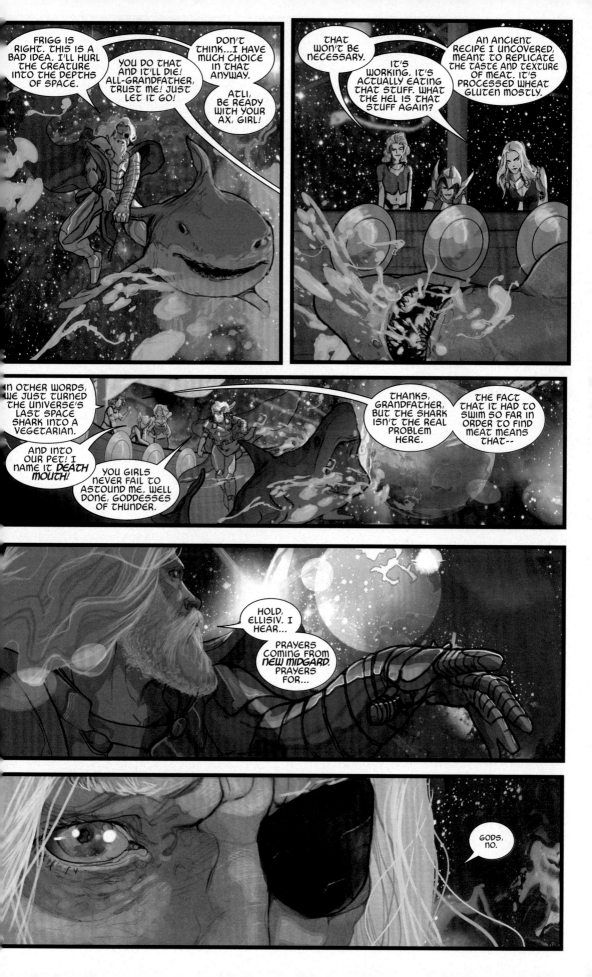

SHE'S BEEN WEAK FOR DAYS. THIS MORNING, SHE COULD NOT RISE AND BEGAN ASKING FOR...

...FOR HER CREATOR.

TELL HER HE HAS COME.

SHE KNOWS.

SHE'S NOT TOO OLD OR DEAD TO FEEL THE PRESENCE OF HER GOD. GREETINGS, MY LORD. PLEASE FORGIVE ME IF I DO NOT RISE.

NONSENSE. YOU'VE EARNED YOUR REST, MY LADY. BUILDING A NEW WORLD FROM NOTHING IS NO EASY TASK.

YOU WERE THE BUILDER. MY HUSBAND AND I MERELY THE CARETAKERS.

I MISS HIM, LORD THOR. I HAVE BEEN TOO LONG WITHOUT MY BEAUTIFUL STEVE.

TOO LONG, PERIOD. TWO HUNDRED SEVENTY-FIVE YEARS IS ENOUGH LIFE FOR ANYONE.

NOT FOR YOU.

NOT IF YOU WISH IT.

JUST AS I ONCE GAVE YOU LIFE, I COULD NOW GIVE YOU MORE. MORE OF MY POWER TO KEEP YOU ALIVE.

JUST SAY THE WORD, LADY JANE, AND YOUR GOD WILL MAKE IT SO.

I SAY THEE...NAY, MY LORD.

A GREAT WOMAN IS DEAD.

TWO HUNDRED AND SEVENTY-FIVE YEARS AGO, I MADE HER FROM DUST AND CLAY. BUT LIKE MOST ANY CHILD, SHE VERY QUICKLY OUTGREW HER PARENT.

SHE BROUGHT LIFE AND LOVE TO WHAT HAD BEEN A DEAD EARTH FOR CENTURIES, IN A WAY I NEVER COULD.

SHE WAS AN ALL-MOTHER. THE VERY LAST ALL-MOTHER.

Z

"THE ODINSON BOYS RIDE AGAIN"

KARNILLA. NORNS BE PRAISED. IT IS GOOD TO SEE YOU. I STILL MOURN FOR YOUR FALL AT THE *NORNKEEP,* MY LADY.*

THOR, DON'T TELL ME *YOU'RE* DEAD, TOO. NOW WE'LL *NEVER* STOP MALEKITH'S WAR.

*MIGHTY THOR #700.

NOT DEAD, MY DEAR QUEEN OF THE NORNS. ONLY VISITING.

WELL, THE DAY IS STILL YOUNG, PRINCE OF LIES. PERHAPS WE'LL GET YOU KILLED OFF YET.

ODINSON REUNION, YOU SAY? HA!

I SUPPOSE IT IS *NOW!*

TYR?

HELLO, LITTLE BROTHER THOR. I SEE YOU'VE STILL GOT THE BEARD OF A SCRAWNY ELF GIRL.

OH, TERRIFIC. *ALL* MY FAVORITE DEAD BROTHERS ARE HERE.

HUG ME LIKE YOU MEAN IT, THUNDER BOY! IT'S NOT LOVE UNLESS BONES ARE CRACKING!

HKK. DEFINITELY... FEELS LIKE LOVE TO ME.

KARNILLA, DID YOU FIND IT?

DID YOU AND TYR UNCOVER THE LOCATION OF SINDR'S SECRET MEETING?

I'M AFRAID NOT, MY LOVE. WE TRIED TO FOLLOW OUR SPY, BUT THE SONS OF MUSPEL WERE TOO CRAFTY AND LOST US IN THE NORTHERN SHADOW LANDS.

WHEREVER THAT MEETING IS HAPPENING...

THE WATERS OF THE GJOLL RIVER ARE CRUSHINGLY COLD AND DEATHLY VENOMOUS.

THE DEEPER I SWIM, THE MORE I FEEL THE LIFE FLOWING OUT OF ME. BUT IF I DIE, I DIE TO END THE WAR.

AND I DO SO GLADLY.

UNTIL I SEE WHAT IT IS WE'VE JUST UNLEASHED. AND THEN I REALIZE...

...WE'VE JUST STARTED ANOTHER WAR OF OUR OWN.

UH-OH. BIG UGLY FISH.

THAT'S NO FISH, THORI...

"A LOVELY DAY IN HEL FOR A WEDDING"

"WAR IS HEL"

THE GATES OF VALHALLA.

"OLD GODS"

"...OLD MAN LOGAN SURE *DON'T*."

WOLVERINE? IS IT...TRULY YOU?

MEMORIES FALL LIKE GRAINS OF SAND THROUGH THE HANDS OF AN OLD GOD.

FALL AND FORM AN ENDLESS BEACH. ONE EVEN THE BRAVEST OF GODS FEARS TO TREAD UPON.

"WOLVERINE." HAVEN'T GONE BY THAT NAME IN A FEW HUNDRED THOUSAND YEARS. BUT YEAH, THOR. IT'S ME.

BY ALL THE BONES OF MY FOREFATHERS. I HAD NO IDEA YOU'D BECOME THE AVATAR OF THE *PHOENIX*.

I THOUGHT THE FIREBIRD HAD PERISHED MANY EONS AGO, WHEN MIDGARD WAS--

--TURNED TO ASH BY YOUR BROTHER? YEAH, IT DID DIE.

SO DID I.

BUT IT'S THE DAMN PHOENIX, AIN'T IT? IT ALWAYS MANAGES TO RISE AGAIN.

WHETHER YOU WANT IT TO OR NOT.

SAND SWIRLS BENEATH THE FEET OF A GOD. AND THOR FEELS THE PAINS OF MEMORY. THIS MAN. THIS WAS HIS *FRIEND*.

THE LAST POD OF *ACANTI* WHALES LEFT IN ALL THE COSMOS HAVE BEEN SWIMMING FOR LIGHT-YEARS, STARVING AND SINGING THEIR DEATH SONG...

...WHILE SEARCHING THE DESOLATE REACHES OF SPACE FOR A STAR TO HURL THEMSELVES INTO, AS IS THEIR WAY.

BUT OUT HERE THERE ARE NO STARS. ONLY DARKNESS.

A DARKNESS THAT *HUNGERS.*

THE LIVING DARKNESS OF EGO THE NECROWORLD.

JOIN *GALACTUS* IN MY MOLTEN GULLET, LITTLE FISHES! GALACTUS AND THE ARMADAS OF THE *KREE'AR EMPIRE* AND THE LAST OF THOSE FUMBLING, INBRED *CELESTIALS!*

NOTHING THAT LIVES IN ALL THE HEAVENS CAN STAND BEFORE EGO!

ONCE, THERE HAD BEEN A SWORD CALLED *ALL-BLACK.*

THE CYCLONE IS THE SIZE OF A SUPERNOVA, SUCKING UP CHUNKS OF DEAD WORLDS FROM PARSECS AWAY.

AND TURNING THEM INTO LIGHTNING-CHARGED COMETS.

IT HAS BEEN YEARS SINCE ALL-FATHER THOR ERUPTED WITH SO MUCH GODLY POWER. IT'S ALMOST ENOUGH TO MAKE HIM SMILE.

ALMOST.

THE PHOENIX RAPTOR STRETCHES FOR LIGHT-YEARS. A FIREBIRD THE SIZE OF A GALAXY. HIS CLAWS BURN HOT ENOUGH TO MELT STARS.

NO LONGER IS HE LOGAN OR EVEN THE PHOENIX. HE IS BECOME A THING MADE SOLELY OF RAGE AND FIRE.

THE COSMIC BERSERKER.

RRRRRRGGGHHH!!!

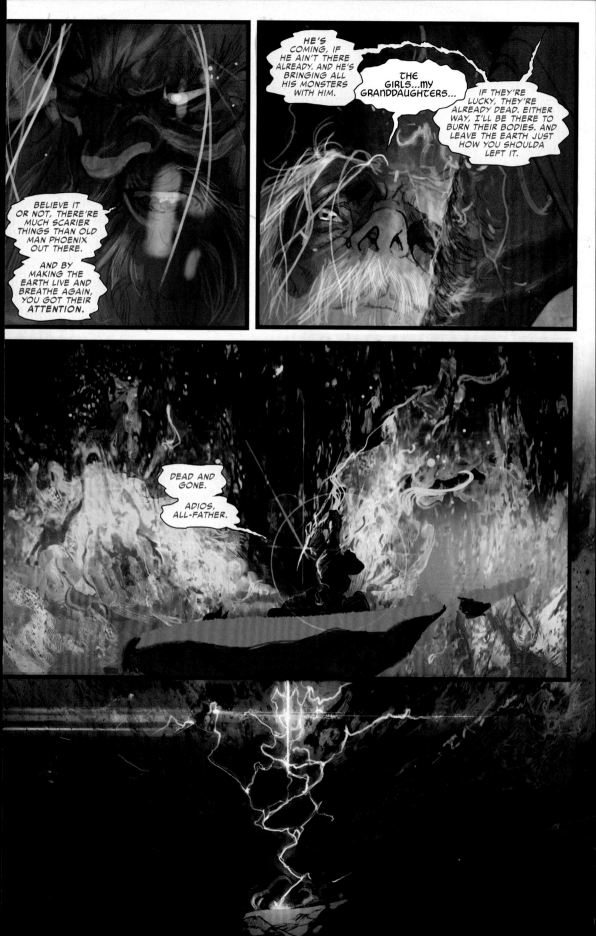

LOOKS LIKE YOUR MINIONS HAVE THEIR HANDS FULL, DRAGON. NOT MUCH OF A MASTER NOW, ARE YOU?

YOU MISUNDERSTAND, CHILD. FIN FANG FOOM IS NOT THE MASTER HERE.

HE IS.

"MIDGARD'S FINAL DOOM"

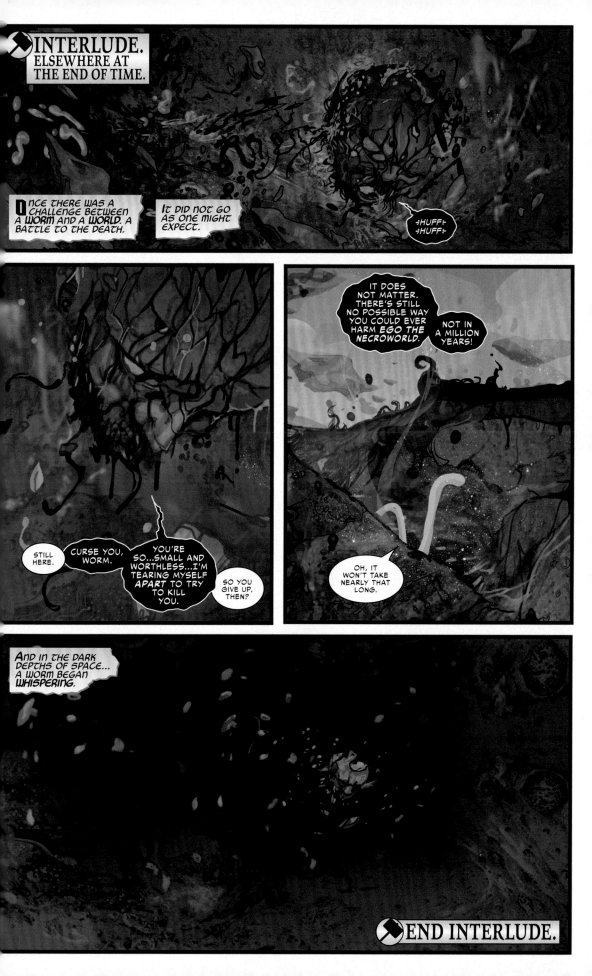

INTERLUDE.
ELSEWHERE AT THE END OF TIME.

ONCE THERE WAS A CHALLENGE BETWEEN A *WORM* AND A *WORLD*. A BATTLE TO THE DEATH.

IT DID NOT GO AS ONE MIGHT EXPECT.

‡HUFF‡
‡HUFF‡

IT DOES NOT MATTER. THERE'S STILL NO POSSIBLE WAY YOU COULD EVER HARM *EGO THE NECROWORLD.*

NOT IN A MILLION YEARS!

STILL HERE.

CURSE YOU, WORM.

YOU'RE SO...SMALL AND WORTHLESS...I'M TEARING MYSELF *APART* TO TRY TO KILL YOU.

SO YOU GIVE UP, THEN?

OH, IT WON'T TAKE NEARLY THAT LONG.

AND IN THE DARK DEPTHS OF SPACE... A WORM BEGAN WHISPERING.

END INTERLUDE.

#1 VARIANT COVER BY ESAD RIBIĆ

#1 VARIANT COVER
BY CHRISTIAN WARD

#1 VARIANT COVER BY JACK KIRBY,
VINCE COLLETTA & PAUL MOUNTS
WITH MICHAEL KELLEHER

#1-5 COMBINED VARIANT COVERS
BY JAMES HARREN & DAVE STEWART

#1 VARIANT COVER
BY KAARE ANDREWS

#1 DESIGN VARIANT COVER
BY RUSSELL DAUTERMAN

#2 VARIANT COVER
BY RUSSEL DAUTERMAN
& MATTHEW WILSON

#2 VARIANT COVER
BY MIKE DEODATO JR.
& FRANK MARTIN

#5 COSMIC GHOST RIDER VS. VARIANT COVER
BY EMA LUPACCHINO
& JASON KEITH

#6 MARVEL KNIGHTS VARIANT COVER
BY RICHARD ISANOVE